Palgrave Macmillan Studies on Human Rights in Asia

Series Editor
Mikyoung Kim, Hiroshima, Japan

This Palgrave Macmillan book series addresses the rising interest in human rights topics in Asia. It focuses on the largely underexplored territory of Asian human rights topics highlighting its empirical manifestations, historical trajectory and theoretical implications. It also goes beyond the problematic dichotomy between "East" and "West" by engaging in rigorous case-specific as well as cross-regional comparisons within South–South context. China's rise in world politics and its emergence as a massive donor, for example, has significant yet troubling implications. The member countries of ASEAN and Northeast Asia, on the other hand, would have different preoccupations and priorities calling for context-sensitive diagnosis and prognosis to promote human right causes.

The series is multidisciplinary in nature and open to submissions focusing on international organization, ethics, criminology, development, freedom of expression, labour rights, environment, human/sex trafficking, democratization, governance studies, disability, reproductive rights, LGBT, post-/colonial as well as post-/authoritarian critiques and social movement, among others.

The series publishes full-length monographs, and edited volumes.

Emma Dalton · Caroline Norma

Voices from the Contemporary Japanese Feminist Movement

palgrave
macmillan

Emma Dalton
Department of Languages
and Cultures
La Trobe University
Melbourne, VIC, Australia

Caroline Norma
School of Global, Urban
and Social Studies
RMIT University
Melbourne, VIC, Australia

ISSN 2752-4310　　　　　　ISSN 2752-4329　(electronic)
Palgrave Macmillan Studies on Human Rights in Asia
ISBN 978-981-19-2227-5　　　ISBN 978-981-19-2228-2　(eBook)
https://doi.org/10.1007/978-981-19-2228-2

© The Author(s), under exclusive license to Springer Nature Singapore Pte Ltd. 2022
This work is subject to copyright. All rights are solely and exclusively licensed by the Publisher, whether the whole or part of the material is concerned, specifically the rights of reprinting, reuse of illustrations, recitation, broadcasting, reproduction on microfilms or in any other physical way, and transmission or information storage and retrieval, electronic adaptation, computer software, or by similar or dissimilar methodology now known or hereafter developed.
The use of general descriptive names, registered names, trademarks, service marks, etc. in this publication does not imply, even in the absence of a specific statement, that such names are exempt from the relevant protective laws and regulations and therefore free for general use.
The publisher, the authors, and the editors are safe to assume that the advice and information in this book are believed to be true and accurate at the date of publication. Neither the publisher nor the authors or the editors give a warranty, expressed or implied, with respect to the material contained herein or for any errors or omissions that may have been made. The publisher remains neutral with regard to jurisdictional claims in published maps and institutional affiliations.

Cover illustration: Bhong-Jin Kim

This Palgrave Macmillan imprint is published by the registered company Springer Nature Singapore Pte Ltd.
The registered company address is: 152 Beach Road, #21-01/04 Gateway East, Singapore 189721, Singapore

Acknowledgements

Although Emma Dalton and Caroline Norma appear as the authors of this book, *Voices from the Contemporary Japanese Feminist Movement* was completed only thanks to the generosity of its contributors. The project would not have been possible without the feminist activists featured in this book—Kitahara Minori, Yamamoto Jun, Nitō Yumeno, Tsunoda Yukiko, Mitsui Mariko, and Yang Ching-Ja. We especially thank the managing director of the feminist publisher etc. books (https://etcbooks.co.jp/), Matsuo Akiko, for her kind permission to translate and include in Chapter 2 the essay published by etc. books in 2019 titled *Konbini kara onna no ero hon ga nakunatta hi*. We also thank its author, Kitahara Minori, for this same kind permission.

Emma would like to thank the members of the Alliance of Feminist Representatives for their longstanding support of and help with all her research endeavours over the last decade and a half. Representatives Aizu Motoko, Katayama Kaoru, and Hinata Misako, to name a few, have extended their kindness and generosity to offer insights into their organisation's activities, motivations, and values. Emma is equally grateful to the director of the Fusae Ichikawa Center for Women and Governance, Kubo Kimiko, whose welcoming and informative conversations over cups of tea in Tokyo have provided endless inspiration. The accumulated knowledge held by, and feminist analyses espoused by the women in these groups underpins almost every chapter in this book.

Caroline would like to thank the members and staff of the Anti-Pornography and Prostitution Research Group (APP), People Against Pornography and Sexual Violence (PAPS), and No!Self-ID Japan.

While writing this book, both Emma and Caroline worked in the School of Global, Urban and Social Studies at RMIT University in Melbourne, Australia. We are fortunate to have enjoyed the support of our colleagues in the Languages and Translating&Interpreting team, particularly during the time of writing when we were physically separated from each other and our colleagues due to various mobility restrictions in the pandemic. Thanks also must go to Hiroko Levy and Emiko Kurata for their help at various stages of the writing and editing process.

We are thankful to the RMIT College Human Ethics Advisory Network, which assessed our project to ensure it upholds ethical integrity and is consistent with the guidelines contained in the Australian National Statement on Ethical Conduct in Human Research and Australian Code for the Responsible Conduct of Research.

Finally, *Voices from the Contemporary Japanese Feminist Movement* ultimately came together thanks to the excellent work of the team at Palgrave Macmillan. Our thanks go to Commissioning Editor, Vishal Daryanomel, who believed in this as a viably interesting project, to Mikyoung Kim, the editor of the Palgrave Macmillan Studies on Human Rights in Asia series, who was similarly enthusiastic about our proposal, and to project coordinators, Aishwarya Balachandar and Aurelia Heumader for bringing it all together.

Japanese-Language Transliteration Conventions Followed in This Book

Japanese names are written with surnames appearing first, unless the individual is being referred to in respect of an English-language publication in which their authorial surname is placed last. Japanese organisational names are transliterated in italics, followed by their English-language translations in brackets. When an organisation has a recognised English-language name, we indicate it in the brackets using first-initial capitals for all major words. When no such name exists, we present the translation in the brackets with a first-initial capital only for the first word. Extended vowels are indicated with macrons except for words that are directly quoted without any original diacritic markings, or when the word is well known to English-language readers.

Contents

1. Introduction: The Modest but Urgent Voices of Contemporary Japanese Feminism ... 1
2. Kitahara Minori: At the Heart of Japan's Feminist Movement of the #MeToo Era ... 15
3. Yamamoto Jun: Survivor-Activist for the Sexually Abused ... 27
4. Nitō Yumeno: Collaborating for the Rights of Teenage Girls ... 39
5. Tsunoda Yukiko: Feminist Activist Lawyer ... 53
6. Mitsui Mariko: A Feminist Leading Feminists ... 69
7. Yang Ching-Ja: Seeds of Hope ... 85
8. Japan's Feminist Movement Within the Global Sisterhood ... 109

References ... 121
Index ... 129

About the Authors

Dalton Emma first studied in Japan in 1995 as an exchange student at a girls' high school in Kobe. She returned to Japan in 1997 as a university exchange student at Kochi University. After obtaining her Ph.D. in Japanese studies from the University of Wollongong, she was a visiting professor at Nagoya City University in 2012 and a lecturer at Kanda University of International Studies for 2 years after that. She has also held research positions at Rikkyo University and Sophia University. She now lectures in Japanese studies at La Trobe University. She researches women's involvement in Japanese electoral politics. Her 2021 publication, *Sexual Harassment in Japanese Politics*, draws on interviews with women politicians to show the sexist conditions in which women at all levels of politics work, and the repercussions of these conditions on women's rights and democracy in Japan.

Norma Caroline first studied in Japan in 1997, and afterwards was a student or researcher at Yamaguchi, Hiroshima, and Doshisha universities. She first met Emma Dalton as a Master of Japanese Interpreting and Translation student at the University of Queensland in 2002. Since 2010, Caroline has lectured in the Master of Translating and Interpreting degree at RMIT University in the Languages and Translating&Interpreting team. Her research focuses on the 'comfort women' Japanese military sexual slavery scheme of World War II, and she collaborates with Morita Seiya in research critical of Japan's contemporary sex industry.

CHAPTER 1

Introduction: The Modest but Urgent Voices of Contemporary Japanese Feminism

Abstract This chapter introduces the feminist activists whose testimonies form the basis of the main 6 chapters of the book. It suggests these testimonies overall show Japan's contemporary feminist movement to be modest and limited, but this characterisation refers to its current influence and reach rather than its future potential. The chapter notes a raft of English-language books already addressing Japan's feminist movement, but not exclusively from the point of view of the activists involved, nor necessarily those involved in the contemporary movement. Insufficient attention and support given this movement by the English-speaking feminist world is lamented, and action by the global feminist movement to rally around local Japanese activists is urged, to support their efforts to stem further decline in the social position of women and girls in Japan, which the chapter describes. While the chapter notes a range of problems these women and girls currently face, it nonetheless suggests the global feminist movement is pivoting towards East Asia.

Keywords Contemporary Japanese feminist movement · #MeToo · #WeToo · Feminist activist · South Korean feminism · COVID-19 pandemic · Itō Shiori · Political alienation among Japanese women · Global feminism · East Asia

© The Author(s), under exclusive license to Springer Nature Singapore Pte Ltd. 2022
E. Dalton and C. Norma, *Voices from the Contemporary Japanese Feminist Movement*, Palgrave Macmillan Studies on Human Rights in Asia,
https://doi.org/10.1007/978-981-19-2228-2_1

The snapshot of a feminist movement in the second decade of the twenty-first century that this book captures is not a triumphal one written as any monument to the success of the #MeToo era in Japan. In fact, as will be shortly explained, feminism did not see a resurgence in Japan from 2016 as it did in other countries. What, then, is the purpose of this book? It describes Japan's grassroots feminist movement of the second decade of the twenty-first century precisely in light of undramatic and inconspicuous developments occurring over 5 years. In other words, the book captures a movement neither in abeyance nor riding high on a sustained wave of feminist radicalism. The contemporary Japanese feminist movement portrayed here remains, at this point, a modest project pursued by committed and well-networked activists who have relatively clear-sighted theoretical views of different aspects of women's condition in the country. While this state of the movement is described in modest and limited terms, these activists do, concurrently, have good comprehension of steps needed to improve both women's condition in Japan and the vitality of the feminist movement itself. So, this book records a feminist movement that remains, at present, a 'work in progress'—to paraphrase Tsunoda Yukiko's assessment in Chapter 5—and whose results are pending, but whose proponents have a great deal of knowledge and experience to contribute to the global feminist movement, including that in countries who have seen greater successes than those of Japan.

Beyond this introductory chapter, this book does not dwell on the failures and insufficiencies of Japan's contemporary feminist movement. To do so would obstruct the sharp insights of the activist testimonies featured, and muddy the picture of the movement they construct through valuable and vivid description. It must be noted, though, for the sake of necessary perspective to be brought to this description, and accurate portrayal of its context, that, compared to other countries, including similarly sex-unequal South Korea, women in Japan face social and political conditions of notable severity. For example, the country's legal sexual age-of-consent remains at 13 years, the percentage of women in non-regular employment is roughly double that of men, single-mother households are substantially poorer on average than in other advanced industrialised countries (Nishimura), there exists no legal consent standard for rape, Japan's sex-based wage gap is now second or third highest in the OECD (Beniyama), the country maintains no sex offenders register, the sex-based division of housework in Japan is second widest in the OECD (Hamada), the sexual assault of underage girls on public transport in Tokyo is near ubiquitous (Makino), the proportion of female science and technology students in Japan is the lowest in the OECD (Suzuki), female political representation is the lowest in the OECD (Dalton), female leadership in Japan's political and corporate worlds is lower than nearly all other OECD countries (Nae), rates of female employment in the public service are among the lowest in the world, pain relief during childbirth is almost never offered to mothers (Doering et al.), and no anti-beauty movement has emerged in Japan like it has in South Korea. Such problems of misogyny do, of course, plague every country in the world, and there are countries where women's situation in some realms are much worse than those of Japan.[1] Even compared to their East Asian sisters, though, women and girls do face measurably worse social and political conditions in Japan, and there are relatively few signs of improvement on the horizon. This situation is not, of course, the fault or responsibility of the country's feminist movement, but it does reflect the movement's lack of influence and reach. Our opinion in this regard is iterated by any number of feminists in Japan, and neither they, nor we, offer such an outlook gladly.[2]

Different from a 2019-edited book, though, we do not attribute this lack of influence and reach to happiness-induced political apathy among the country's female population. In *Beyond the Gender Gap*, Gill Steel argues that, despite living in conditions of sex inequality, Japanese women are 'not angry' (16), they prefer shopping to protesting (11), and craft individualised solutions to systemic problems rather than organise politically (3). Certainly, only a small minority of women in Japan call themselves feminist, an even smaller minority is involved in feminist activism, and the label feminist has negative connotations that most

---

[1] In India, for example, marital rape is not yet outlawed. The age of sexual consent in some jurisdictions in the US is 16, and in France is only 15. In our own country, Australia, the pay gap between men and women fulltime workers exceeds 14 per cent, and for all workers is a startlingly high 30 per cent. Australia, like other Western countries, exercises judicial policies that discriminate against, and often seriously endanger, divorced women and their children in the name of 'fathers' rights', and ideas about male prerogative in maintaining access to children irrespective of violence against wives, and even the children themselves.

[2] We recommend to readers with heavy hearts recent books describing the frightening extent to which women's social condition in Japan is declining, such as Junko Nishimura's 2016 *Motherhood and Work in Contemporary Japan*, and Fujita Takanori's 2021 *Korona Hinkon: Zetsubōteki Kakusa Shakai no Shūrai*.

women eschew for its extremism, selfishness, and man-hatred (Bulbeck 71; Dales, 'Feminist Futures in Japan Exploring the Work of Haruka Yoko and Kitahara Minori' 185). Political alienation among women, though, is not logically a cause but a symptom of the success of Japanese men in mobilising their countrywomen in service of their own interests as men, and for male purposes. This success can be explained historically (see Norma, *Comfort Women and Post-Occupation Corporate Japan*), but is not here. It suffices to note that the male sex class domination of women and girls in Japan is near-impeachable in some areas: for example, men block women's entry to labour market sectors with decent pay and conditions more thoroughly in Japan than any other 'advanced industrialised' country in the world (see Hashimoto). A more personalised illustration of this absolutist male power arises in the case of the survivor most responsible for the spread of #MeToo in Japan from 2017. Journalist Itō Shiori was raped and brutally assaulted by a high-profile fellow journalist, but these facts were recognised only in a later civil court case that Itō was forced to launch after her many and dogged attempts to pursue her attacker criminally were obstructed and thwarted over many years by the police, the courts, and Japan's media. The extraordinary hardships of Itō's case are captured in a 2017 book (translated into English in 2021) that describes unresponsiveness even from rape crisis services and the medical profession (Itō). In spite of the injustice and severity of her case, moreover, no subsequent domino effect of public outrage at men in entertainment and cultural industries taking advantage of positions to assault and harass female underlings, as was the tendency of #MeToo movements in other parts of the world, arose in Japan.

Reasons given by Japanese feminists for this comparatively subdued response echo our view of the magnitude of the male power that reigns in Japan, and the extent of the obstruction it poses to the social progress of women and girls. Muta Kazue (37), for example, suggests that backlash awaits women who speak out about sexual abuse in Japan, and this causes the movement's restraint. She suggests further that sexual harassment and sexual violence are simply not concepts widely understood by the general public. This meant that an indigenous #MeToo uprising—even if it had occurred on a small scale in Japan—would not have been supported by the media, and would therefore have struggled to permeate public consciousness as it did in other countries. Kitahara Minori in 2021 similarly noted punishment awaiting victims who speak up in Japan: 'How many times have we stood back and watched women face heartless attacks when they step forward as victims? Women can't be anything but scared to speak up in a society where this happens. There's no chance #MeToo would have succeeded in such a society' ('Hajimatta Furawā Demo' 22). From a similar, but more middle-class point of view, Ki-young Shin (54–55) suggests that, when it comes to sexual harassment, Japanese women refrain from speaking up because they do not want to ruin their careers or make their lives difficult at work. In response to this environment, in a spirit of solidarity with victims, and as a way to protect bystander anonymity, women galvanised around the alternative social media slogan #WeToo, rather than #MeToo, with the former slogan intended to reassure victims they had allies. Nonetheless, Linda Hasunuma and Ki-young Shin (106) argue that even the uptake of this slogan shows how, compared to other countries, sexual harassment remains a private problem in Japan because of powerful cultural norms that pressure people to not speak out against wrongdoings so as to maintain group harmony. In their view, this pressure to conform places a particularly heavy burden on women who are the targets of most sexual violence.

We might lament the fact that large female populations all over the world are not yet mobilised as feminists, and so prefer shopping to protest, as Steel notes of Japanese women, but, as Catharine MacKinnon's 2019 *Butterfly Politics: Changing the World for Women* shows, this situation is neither inexorable nor immutable, and can in fact change overnight. Analyses that suggest Japanese women are a population impervious to political change are, at the very least, historically naive, given evidence of, for example, the efforts of pre-war Japanese women in achieving changes like the *Prostitution Prevention Law* in 1956 (see Shibahara). We further wonder where the confidence for such proclamations on Japanese women comes from, given the feminist uprising in South Korea that has been continuing since 2016, which is a country geographically close, and similar, to Japan in many ways. Thankfully, the 6 testimonies of this book show that political conditions are maintained in Japan, in terms of networks and theoretical analyses, that are conducive to supporting future feminist resurgence. While the movement does not succeed in Japan at present, the maintenance of these analyses, campaigns, and projects of significant feminist organisation and networking, which are described in the 6 ensuing chapters, show that, no matter what the current political state, as conditions shift and possibilities open up, feminism has a chance in Japan. Even if very modest and limited, the country's feminist movement stands ready and able to support its growth.

While we describe here Japan's contemporary feminist movement as modest and limited, at the same time we believe there is no more urgent and pressing time for the global feminist movement to turn its attention to Japanese voices, show interest in, and lend support to, the country's women's movement. The severity of the sex-differentiated impact of the pandemic over the years 2020 and 2021 showed the need for feminist mobilisation in Japan perhaps more acutely than any other country. Women and girls found themselves at the mercy of a society ill-equipped to respond to the needs of women and children in particular. These groups became responsible for infection prevention measures after a snap three-month school closure policy was announced in the absence of any wider social lockdown. Partly as a result, because of women leaving or reducing employment to take care of children, a poverty relief organisation operating for decades in the western city of Otsu suggested in December 2021 that rates of female immiseration in Japan were at levels not seen since the country's post-war reconstruction ('Josei No Seikatsu Konkyū Wa "Sengo Saiaku" 70-Nen Ijō Shien Shitekita Shiga/Otsu-Shi No Shien Dantai Ga Tsutaetai Koto'). A 2021 research paper by Zhou Yanfei showed that, by mid-2020, 'female employees who are raising children under the age of 18 are in particularly disadvantageous circumstance[s]', and '[f]emales are three to four times more likely to be on furlough than male[s]', because industries targeted for closure in the pandemic (involving hospitality and tourism) are more likely to employ non-regular women workers. Whether due to sudden poverty or greater contact with abusive partners, female suicide soared in the pandemic, especially among young women, and domestic violence reports—mostly to civic organisations rather than police—skyrocketed (Ando). Appeals for help from women trapped in the prostitution and pornography industries so overwhelmed NGOs in Tokyo that the backlog of phone calls is only now, 2 years into the pandemic, beginning to be addressed (Norma, 'FiLiA'). The sex-specific nature of the problems arising in Japan during the pandemic cannot be too alarmingly described, but if there were any bright side, they at least show that social progress will be disproportionately responsive to feminist agitation in Japan. Global feminist interest in, and support of, local efforts to promote this agitation are, though, greatly needed, given the dire lack of resources and institutional bases upon which activists in Japan attempt to improve the condition of women and girls.

On a shoestring, a broad-spanning feminist movement does operate in Japan, even if this book, for logistical and space-related reasons, fails to capture all the individuals and feminist organisations that, in aggregate, make up a movement that covers a broad range of problems of sexism. For example, prostitution and pornography (People Against Pornography and Sexual Violence (PAPS) and the Anti-Pornography and Prostitution Research Group (APP)) (see Norma and Morita), sexual assault (the now-defunct Osaka Women Against Sexual Assault), child custody rights for mothers after divorce (supported by Musashino University academic Senda Yūki), female social and political leadership (Ichikawa Fusae Center for Women and Governance), and the sexual abuse of students by male teachers (Ishida Ikuko and her #Schoolmetoo campaign). The testimonies incorporated in this book from 6 feminist activists were selected for the comprehensiveness of the account they collectively generate, within space constraints, of Japan's contemporary feminist movement. There will always be limits on the scope of this picture, of course, and little mention is made in these pages of umbrella organisations like Women's Action Network (WAN), Women's Active Museum on War and Peace (WAM), or the Asia-Japan Women's Resource Center (AJWRC) that operate in Japan, but mainly as clearinghouses for feminist scholarship and documentation. Most derelict is our failure to include feminist activists campaigning against domestic violence. Nor do we include any individuals or organisations based outside of Tokyo. The 6 activists included nonetheless all represent either one specific feminist organisation, or are closely connected to a number of currently active feminist organisations. Each are 'feminist activists' in the sense they understand their political activity to be specifically feminist, and in this selection criterion, the current book is different from Laura Dales' 2009 *Feminist Movements in Contemporary Japan*, which focuses on women's activism not necessarily recognised by its proponents as feminist. The women included in this book are, moreover, specifically activists rather than academics or NGO workers. They are prioritised over academics, even of an activist variety, not just because of their lesser heard voices, but because we view with consternation the widening ideological and campaigning distance between grassroots feminist activity and academia around the world, including in Japan. We note this distance has become a problem of escalating proportions with the onset of debates over 'gender identity', and these debates currently produce fissures even among academic feminists in Japan.[3] One of the contributors to this book, Kitahara Minori, underscores this longstanding cleavage between academicfeminists and feministactivists in the context of explaining her own feminist evolution:

> Feminists are not supposed to be people who go around preaching politically correct things, they are supposed to be the fighters of this society: tackling head-on problems of sexuality. But the time that I found myself mired in the problems of sexuality of Japanese society [at the time of an obscenity charge, see Chapter 2], the people in academia working under the banner of feminism were the ones who most stuck to politically correct responses and didn't support me…This made me question what direction I wanted to take my feminism in. (Kitahara and Satō 25–26)

By introducing testimony from 6 women who represent different feminist organisations, all of which centrally address problems facing women and girls, this book paints a picture of the Japanese feminist movement at the same time as generating insights about some of the most serious problems facing women and girls in the country. These problems are current as well as historical. Contemporary survivors of sexual violence are represented by Kitahara Minori in Chapter 2 who describes the so-called 'Flower demo' campaign that developed in Japan in the #MeToo era in support of victims. Chapter 3, incorporating testimony from Yamamoto Jun of the organisation Spring, similarly focuses on grassroots feminist efforts to achieve legislative reform for sexual violence survivors. The sexual exploitation of teenage girls is discussed by the founder and director of the organisation Colabo, Nitō Yumeno, in Chapter 4. A focus on legal change emerges again in Chapter 5 with Tsunoda Yukiko's account of feminist efforts against sexual harassment. The sex inequality that is embedded in legal and judicial practices and systems in Japan, as well as the dearth of women in political decision-making roles, is described by Mitsui Mariko in Chapter 6. Lastly, Yang Ching-Ja in Chapter 7 describes efforts to support sexual slavery survivors commonly known as 'comfort women' who were victimised by the Japanese military in the Second World War. The concluding chapter refocuses on South Korea's feminist activism and discusses the success of South Korean

---

[3] Such as debates occurring within the Women's Studies Association of Japan.

feminism since 2016, which forms an important practical and ideological backdrop to the contemporary Japanese feminist movement.

Other 'Voices' of Japanese Women

The key phrase in the title of this book might be familiar to readers. A number of books have already been written on the topic of 'feminism in Japan'; most prominently, the 1996 collection of essays compiled by the *Japan-Asia Quarterly Review* journal titled *Voices from the Japanese Women's Movement* (Ampo Japan-Asia Quarterly Review) which incorporates chapters written exclusively by Japanese women, among whom are well-known feminist theorists and activists such as Kanai Yoshiko, Ehara Yumiko, Inoue Reiko, Kim Puja, and Hayashi Yoko. This 25-year-old publication (released in a second edition with a new introduction in 2015) adopts a radical definition of feminism as focused on conditions of women's sex-based oppression and activism needed to tackle them, both of which guide the discussion of this book too. *Voices From the Japanese Women's Movement* discusses issues facing Japanese women in the 1980s and 1990s, the feminist activism happening at the time, and the ideological debates that underpinned this activism. Theoretically animated by the radical feminism that was relatively widespread in countries in the West in the 1980s, the authors critique Japanese feminism for its *lack of* radicalism, and argue for a move away from 'housewife feminism', which, they argue, was failing to challenge unequal power relations between women, and neglected issues of sexuality (Kanai), at the time. While this book does not follow a similar format, in that its chapters are not written directly by Japanese women themselves, it nonetheless inherits both its political perspective as well as its commitment to recording the perspectives of Japanese feminists, on their movement as well as on issues of sexism, *in their own words*.

The following year, in 1997, Sandra Buckley published *Broken Silence: Voices of Japanese Feminism* while holding a professorial appointment at a university in Australia. Buckley interviewed 10 Japanese feminists in the late 1980s, and compiled these translated interview transcripts (including her questions to the interviewees) alongside one translated piece of writing from each interviewee. Different from the current book, her interviewees seem to have been selected not on the basis of their activist histories or ties to feminist organisations, but, rather, their contribution to the 'rich cacophony of voices constantly redefining and renegotiating the boundaries of feminism' in Japan (p. xviii). Buckley's interest in interviewing and translating the work of the 10 women was to capture a spectrum of feminist thought circulating in Japan at the time rather than necessarily to depict the country's feminist movement. So, even though Buckley's volume is similar to the current one in its transcription of interviews with feminists, like other works in the 'voices of Japanese feminism' category it focuses on their feminist ideas rather than grassroots action. This difference notwithstanding, the format and spirit of the current book owes a great deal to the groundbreaking blueprint established by Buckley for investigating contemporary Japanese feminism. Placed alongside her compilation, it serves as a comparator for change occurring in Japanese feminism over 3 decades. Revisiting Buckley's book, we were surprised to realise, for example, how much sexual exploitation continues to preoccupy Japanese feminists.

Ueno's English-language book-chapter published in 2019 as part of a compendium titled the *Routledge Handbook of East Asian Gender Studies* is, however, more different than similar to earlier volumes in its view of feminism and circumstances of female lives. Ueno's view is that improvements in women's condition have been achieved on all fronts in Japan. Some of the specifics of this optimistic assessment are at odds with claims made in the current book, such as the 'illegality' of '*chikan*' sexual assault on public transport, and the sufficiency of coverage of services catering to women fleeing domestic violence in Japan. But, whatever these details, Ueno is most concerned to applaud Japan's feminist movement as having become one of multiple 'feminisms', and as having overcome the 'gender essentialism' of the 1980s to embrace 'minority feminisms'. Indeed, more than gains made for Japan's most vulnerable women and girls, it is often this alleged achievement of inclusion and diversity by Japan's feminist movement that is nominated by writers who reflect upon its history as its most praiseworthy feature. This aim is frequently and inexplicably assumed to preoccupy the movement, and was similarly celebrated in an earlier volume, published in 2011, titled *Transforming Japan: How Feminism and Diversity Are Making a Difference* by Kumiko Fujimura-Fanselow. Like Ueno, Fujimura-Fanselow takes as her measure of the prosperity and success of Japan's feminist movement the extent to which it maintains a diffused focus on a range of issues, most of which pertain not solely to women and girls. Paradoxically, though, in parallel to this favourable assessment of the movement, she notes declining conditions of women's social position in Japan at the turn of the twenty-first century, and remarks that, compared to the 1990s, 'the picture is less rosy' for women, and 'there is little progress to be seen'. On the contrary, according to Fujimura-Fanselow, 'one sees regression in aspects of Japanese women's lives' (20).

Titles that include reference to 'Japanese feminism' alternatively perceive of the movement as predominantly a phenomenon of history, and broach discussion of contemporary activists and organisations only after, and only briefly, at their discussion's end. Vera Mackie's 2003 *Feminism in Modern Japan* describes issues that have exercised the Japanese feminist movement since the late 1800s, including suffrage, sexuality, international women's movements, and participation in political and public life. Mackie's discussion focuses mostly on historical approaches taken by women's groups to these issues, but her discussion does draw on conversations with contemporary feminist activists, and, in this respect, captures some picture of 'contemporary Japanese feminism'. But this comes only after, and only briefly, at the book's end. Contemporary Japanese feminist activism is even less addressed in the 2017 edited *Rethinking Japanese Feminisms* (Welker et al.), which explores myriad themes, including the question of 'what constitutes feminism'. Answers proposed tend to be impossible to pin down, and the book's contributors explore well-known academic and literary feminist topics, such as the enduring Japanese ideology of 'good wife, wise mother'. A small number of chapters do assess aspects of Japan's feminist movement since the 1970s, but they are not written by movement proponents. Ayako Kano's 2016 *Japanese Feminist Debates: A Century of Contention on Sex, Love, and Labor* is similarly focused on ideas of Japanese feminism rather than political action taken on their basis. Kano suggests that Japanese feminism is most lively in written form, rather than in effecting immediate or obvious social change, and so her focus is on printed feminist debates rather than real-life activism. Kano, as an academic at the University of Pennsylvania, is not necessarily a participant in the social movement that generates and pursues these debates, moreover, and her discussion does not incorporate much of their proponents' own words.

More similar to this book are a number of Japanese-language publications released in the #MeToo era that examine contemporary feminist activism in Japan, and the sex-unequal conditions under which this activism is pursued. A recent example is *Nihon No Feminizumu Since 1886* (Japanese feminism since 1886), edited by Kitahara Minori in 2017, which surveys historical and contemporary debates and activism surrounding women's sex-based rights in Japan, and the oppression of women by men on the basis, specifically, of sexuality. Contributors are mostly activist scholars, including Onozawa Akane and Taniguchi Mayumi, and their chapters cover problems of prostitution, female reproduction, the history of lesbianism, and women's struggle for sexual self-determination and against sexual exploitation. The compilation also includes writing by grassroots activists and writers, such as Nitō Yumeno (see also Chapter 4 of this book). The overall thesis of Kitahara's edited volume reflects her approach to feminism: that sex-based oppression is primarily a force of sexuality and the oppression of women by men through sex. Indeed, the subtitle of the book is 'Battle of the Sexes Edition' (*Sei no Tatakai Hen*). Kitahara counters arguments by feminists that have, through a modern lens, dismissed one of Japan's first women's organisations, *Kyōfukai* (Christian Women's Temperance Union, formed in 1886), as 'conservative', and she enjoins readers to historically reinterpret the organisation as one that was powerfully women-centred and decidedly feminist in its activities to support single mothers and assist those in the sex trade and those who wanted to leave it (Kitahara, *Nihon No Feminizumu Since 1886* 163).

While we had no knowledge of its upcoming publication before it was released in late 2021, a Japanese-language edited volume titled *Watashi wa Damaranai: Sei Bōryoku wo Nakusu 30 no Shiten* (I Will Not be Silent: 30 Views on Eradicating Sexual Violence) incorporates chapters by Yamamoto Jun (see Chapter 3), Kitahara Minori (see Chapter 2), Nitō Yumeno (see Chapter 4), and Yang Ching-Ja (see Chapter 7), who are all featured in this book (Gōdō Shuppan). Not surprisingly, each of their 4 chapters in the Japanese-language volume are written precisely on the same themes that their testimonies address in this book. The Japanese-language book impressively features 30, and not 6, contributors, even if the chapters are short. While much like this volume the chapters focus on problems of sexual violence, this violence is discussed in relation to not only women and girls, but more broadly 'sexual minorities' and men. While there is much overlapping content between the two volumes—even if written in different languages—we are reassured by this competing publication, at least for the confidence it gives us to say that the activists incorporated in this book are recognised at the grassroots level in Japan as major figures in the country's feminist movement.

Conclusion

We present transcribed and translated verbal testimony of these figures, as well as translated portions of their writings, in the 6 chapters that follow. Each chapter is overlaid with a preface that aims to introduce the contributor and her field of activism, as well as clarify any topics she addresses that need explanation in advance. The contributors discuss both their fields of activism—for example, the 'comfort women'—as well as the feminist groups and individuals involved. In this respect, the testimonies overall produce a picture of women's condition in Japan in terms of the problems of sexism facing its female population, but this picture is shaped by the activism that identifies and defines these problems. Accordingly, the 'contemporary Japanese feminist movement' that is captured in this book is necessarily skewed by the selection of its contributors, as well as the nature of the organisations active at the grassroots that are currently prominent. Whatever its limitations, the eminent insider view of Japan's feminist movement afforded by the discussion of the following 6 chapters likely equips readers with insight enough to begin to make comparisons, or notice patterns, in the twenty-first-century development of global feminism that finds, we believe, its axis increasingly tilted towards East Asia (see, for example, Xue and Rose).

CHAPTER 2

Kitahara Minori: At the Heart of Japan's Feminist Movement of the #MeToo Era

Abstract This chapter discusses the main instigator of the so-called 'Flower demo' movement, including her background running a female-oriented business, and her view of feminism as fundamentally a movement addressing sexuality. Kitahara Minori is a prolific writer, and in her writing reflects upon the evolution in her understanding of feminism over the past 25 years. One piece of writing, published in 2019, translated in this chapter, explores Kitahara's feelings about Japanese convenience stores discontinuing their stocking of pornographic magazines, which she had once objected to when it was female-orientated magazines that were discontinued. This translated piece is followed by a transcription of a speech Kitahara gave on the occasion of the first 'Flower demo' event of 2021. In this speech she reflects on the substantial impact that survivors speaking out about sexual violence has had on Japanese society since the start of 'Flower demo' events in 2019.

Keywords Kitahara Minori · Love Piece Club · 'Flower demo' · #MeToo in Japan · #WeToo · Medical school discrimination · Sexuality as central to feminism · Political transformation · Pornographic magazines in convenience stores · Victims' voices · Sexual violence court cases · COVID-19 pandemic

© The Author(s), under exclusive license to Springer Nature Singapore Pte Ltd. 2022
E. Dalton and C. Norma, *Voices from the Contemporary Japanese Feminist Movement*, Palgrave Macmillan Studies on Human Rights in Asia, https://doi.org/10.1007/978-981-19-2228-2_2

Kitahara Minori is perhaps Japan's best-known feminist of the #MeToo era. She writes prolifically for women-orientated publications such as AERA, the *Asahi Shimbun*-published lifestyle magazine, has a regular column with the same newspaper, and publishes for wider audiences, such as readers of the *Mainichi Shimbun*. Even before the #MeToo era, Kitahara had produced a number of volumes of feminist essays, including the well-known 2014 *Okusama wa Aikoku* (Madam is Patriotism). Most prominently, she was one of the instigators of the so-called 'Flower demo' movement, which involves monthly public speak-out gatherings of sexual assault survivors and their supporters. As Kitahara has noted though, there are no official 'leaders' of this movement ('Hirogaru Furawā Demo' 18), which developed as a broad-based anti-sexual violence campaign in response to a series of 4 sex crime acquittals in March 2019 that attracted attention among women on social media through careful reporting by female journalists. These egregious court judgements emerged *after* some change in cultural norms and beliefs concerning sexual relations between men and women had begun in Japan with the emergence of #MeToo. Itō Shiori's *Black Box* was published in late 2017, and revisions to sex offence provisions in Japan's Penal Code were made in the same year.

As Kitahara wrote in 2021, however, the #MeToo movement failed to take off in Japan because powerful men, such as prominent male lawyers, publicly accuse women of 'becoming too emotional' or 'not knowing anything about the legal system' when they object even to the highly questionable decisions of judges in sex offence cases where, for example, a father was found not guilty even while the court recognised his serial rape of his daughter before she was age 12 ('Hajimatta Furawā Demo' 21). In reaction to this kind of male attack upon female resistance, the 'Flower demo' movement developed and organised explicitly under a campaign slogan of women speaking out in support of survivors 'who must not be abandoned any further to their own isolation', and doing so 'regardless of what men think' ('Hajimatta Furawā Demo' 24). 'Flower demo' protests are convened in all of Japan's prefectures, and, in Tokyo at least, and outside of the pandemic months, they occur monthly, and are attended by supporters like Itō Shiori, Kitahara herself, Yamamoto Jun (see Chapter 3), and politicians from the Japan Communist Party.

As mentioned, this protest movement emerged in the context of the broader #MeToo era, which was a phenomenon of feminist uprising both internationally and locally. By 2019, when the protest events began, women in Japan had already started speaking out about their experiences of workplace harassment and sexual violence. One of the first to do so was a woman who goes by the pseudonym 'Hāchū'. In late 2017, she posted a blog complaining of sexual harassment by her manager at Japan's largest advertising company Dentsu. The manager, Kishi Yūki, admitted to having harassed her 8 years earlier, and stepped down from his position. While Hāchū's public appeal was successful in terms of her perpetrator losing employment, even if not attracting criminal sanction, less publicly explosive in mid-2018 were revelations of Tokyo Medical University having discriminated against female student applicants. The university was found to have altered the entrance examination scores of female candidates to hold down their enrolment numbers. University administrators justified this action on the belief that there would be a shortfall in doctors if too many women became qualified, because they typically gave up careers after marriage and childbirth. A subsequent national inquiry discovered several other universities similarly operating negative quotas against female applicants (Yajima and Masutani). Kitahara reached out to women expressing outrage after realising they had likely been robbed of careers in medicine, and organised a modest public protest outside the university.

This early attempt at feminist organising prefaced Kitahara's subsequent success in instigating the 'Flower demo' campaign. Crucial to this success were her vast networks among women in Japan's civil society, which, by the second decade of the twenty-first century, included political organisations, NGOs, as well as individual writers, academics, and journalists, all of whom Kitahara had been engaged with for several years. For example, she first met Nitō Yumeno (see Chapter 4) and Colabo staff through appearing in a production of Vagina Monologues[1] in Tokyo, which raised funds for Colabo in 2015 (Kitahara and Satō 216).

While the 'Flower demo' campaign achieved success in terms of take-up among groups of women all over Japan, Japanese mainstream media was not as responsive, according to Kitahara, who describes having been disappointed at the fact that, despite having contacted journalists before the first event in Tokyo in 2019, the story was not covered (Nakagawa).

---

[1] The Vagina Monologues is a play written by Eve Ensler, first performed in 1996. After performing it, Ensler was inspired to start the worldwide 'V-Day campaign', which invites communities to perform the Vagina Monologues with the aim of raising awareness of and funds for eradicating violence against women.

The barrier that women face in Japan in terms of mainstream media hostility to feminist perspectives is certainly another factor in the relative lack of success of #MeToo in the country. Itō Shiori's perpetrator had been employed by the Tokyo Broadcasting System (TBS), so her case wasn't covered by that major media outlet in Japan. Male journalists have a reputation for focusing on the nature of the sexual harm experienced by victims at the expense of the criminality of their perpetrators, as Kitahara recently noted in related to former Kusatsu councillor Arai Shōko's case (Kitahara, 'Seihigai Wo Kokuso Shita Moto Kusatsu Chōgi No Josei Ga Kaiken: Kaijō No Kanshin to #MeToo No Zure Ni Shōgeki Wo Uketa'; For details of the case, see Norma and Dalton).

Kitahara's feminist activism has substantial providence, and her first book of feminist essays, *Busu No Hirakinaori* (Defiantly Ugly Women), was published in 2004. She was born in Kanagawa in 1970, and graduated from the prestigious women's university Tsuda University after commencing an international relations major in 1989. She founded her Love Piece Club business in 1996 at age 26, and this online retailer, together with a number of spin-off enterprises, employs over a dozen women and operates today in both Tokyo and Osaka. Love Piece Club originated as a bricks-and-mortar seller of sex-orientated goods, but Kitahara today describes it as a seller of women's 'sexual health products'. Indeed, the business now operates as a female space where women are invited to celebrate and explore female sexual pleasure through awareness-raising, connection-forming, and sex toy consumption. Pornography is no longer sold through the business, after Kitahara decided more than a decade ago to discontinue this product line out of opposition to the sex industry. Today, Love Piece Club is a notably innovative business that functions not just as an online retailer but also as a web-based platform that hosts radio and video series, blogs and chat rooms, as well as a feminist publisher operating under the name Ajuma Books.

The stress of staying financially afloat over the pandemic years is not the only challenge Kitahara has faced in managing her business. In 2014, she was arrested and detained for 3 days after allowing a friend, the artist Igarashi Megumi (professionally known as Rokudenashiko), to leave overnight at the Love Piece Club office one of her outsized artworks. Because this item was a vulva-shaped kayak, it was deemed in breach of Japan's obscenity law, and Kitahara, together with Igarashi, were arrested for supposedly exhibiting the artwork. The incident subsequently caused Kitahara to become disenchanted with Japan's leftist media when they criticised her for not appealing the conviction. (To have done so would have involved too much time and effort spent away from her business and activist activities, Kitahara says.) Kitahara's three-day police detention was a harrowing event in her life, which she subsequently reflected on in a volume written with Satō Masaru in relation to, among other things, the effect of the experience on her commitment to the 'comfort women' issue (see Chapter 7):

> I got involved in the 'comfort women' issue from 2013 when Osaka mayor Hashimoto [Toru] made his public comments about their [wartime] 'necessity', and right-wing groups stepped up their attacks on survivors. But it was only after I was arrested [in 2014] that I came to be more seriously concerned about such issues of bodily integrity like those pertaining to the 'comfort women' issue. This was because I experienced being locked in from the outside as really scary. Being detained and having one's freedom taken away or limited is terrible to even think about. I was detained for just three days, but over a number of hours I was transported in silence while being tied with ropes to ten other people. It's hard to breathe just thinking about it now...It's the trauma of having been restricted that I can't erase from my mind or body even now. [i.e., Kitahara was detained in a small room with 10 other people for 24 hours.] (Kitahara and Satō 121)

Kitahara's gradual move away from the traditional left, and towards more radical forms of feminism, was perhaps unavoidable for her: while working in the physical premises of Love Piece Club in its early days, she would find herself having to fulfil a role of on-the-spot counsellor for women who, finding themselves in a novel environment that was not only a women-only space, but one where they could talk freely about sex, would break down in tears and share stories of sexual abuse (Dales 94). The shift might further have been driven by her increasingly critical approach to the sex industry. Kitahara has certainly maintained a critical viewpoint over decades—she attended an event of the Anti-Pornography and Prostitution Research Group in 1999—but this viewpoint has increasingly been expressed in her activism, as is clear in her appointment to the vice chair of the board of the organisation People Against Pornography and Sexual Violence (PAPS) (https://www.paps.jp/member). Kitahara's feminist approach increasingly focuses on sexuality as a problem to be addressed in Japan. She writes that, '[t]he more our struggles are connected to sexuality, the harder they are. This is because they are not about civic rights, but about issues that men consider natural, cultural, and historical...so they attract male dismissal or mockery' (Kitahara and Satō 250). In efforts to overcome this male dismissiveness, Kitahara has done a lot to rehabilitate the historical reputation of the organisation *Kyōfukai* (Christian Women's Temperance Union), which was formed by Japanese women in pre-war Japan who were against prostitution and other forms of male violence and excess. In her 2017 book *Nihon no Feminizumu since 1886* (Japanese feminism) (163) she praises these women for having spoken up against harms of male sexuality at a time when doing so risked their lives.

This political transformation is described concisely by Kitahara herself in a short book chapter published in 2019 ('Konbini Kara Onna No Ero Hon Ga Nakunatta Hi') about the banishing in the same year of pornographic magazines from Japanese convenience stores. A translation of that piece of writing follows this introduction, and, after that, is a transcribed speech that Kitahara gave in January 2021 to mark the first 'Flower demo' event for that year. While the 2 authors were unable to attend this event, they have both attended 'Flower demo' events in Tokyo and Osaka, and the second author has collaborated with Kitahara over a number of years through their joint involvement in People Against Pornography and Sexual Violence (PAPS), including via an edited volume about PAPS published by Iwanami Shoten in 2021 and edited by Nakasatomi Hiroshi.

THE DAY PORNOGRAPHIC MAGAZINES DISAPPEAR FROM CONVENIENCE STORES

In the early 1990s, when it was completely normal for convenience stores in Japan to sell pornographic magazines, they also sold pornographic magazines 'for women'. These garnered much public attention—like the very famous ladies' comic *Amour*, created by female manga artists using evocative sexual expression, or magazines advertising 'sex with male porn stars!' These lined the shelves of convenience stores. Or at least I think they did... I catch myself as I write this, questioning the accuracy of my memory. As I greet the news that adult magazines will be removed from convenience stores in 2019 in a celebratory mood, I can barely conceive of who I was years ago, back when I would stand in convenience stores reading the pornographic magazines (for women) hoping they would sell well, and I'm a little worried that my memory is deceiving me about the existence of women's pornographic magazines in convenience stores.

But no, they were definitely there! In the mid-1990s, pornography for women spread commercially at a tremendous pace. Women can be subjective consumers of porn *just like men* was the message, and my starting a women's sex shop in 1996 should be understood in this context.

I don't deny all of it, but looking back, I see that period as one of numbness. For example, when people talked about 'compensated dating' (*enjo kōsai*), they weren't talking about the problem of men buying girls, but instead were framing it as a revolution for girls who were exercising their right to sexual self-determination. In the early 1990s, women's sexuality was so repressed that maybe society wanted a new narrative about 'strong and liberated women'.

I don't know when it was that I lost that feeling. I don't clearly remember the day that women's pornographic magazines disappeared from convenience stores, but I remember editors blurting out, 'We've been discontinued. What a shame we can't get into convenience stores anymore'. It was during the [Tokyo] Ishihara [Shintarō] administration, and I think it was just prior to pornographic magazines in convenience stores having to be placed in partitioned areas. So, men's pornographic magazines were relocated and covered in plastic, while women's pornographic magazines were killed off altogether. Since then, women's pornographic magazines haven't been sold at convenience stores; in fact, in Japan in 2019, it's as if they never existed.

Sexual discrimination is embedded into the fabric of society and is constantly reproduced. So, if we only chase after the sexual discrimination right in front of us, not only will we be unable able to keep up with it, we might also be chasing the wrong enemy. With this in mind, I think about the history of porno magazines. The 'unfairness' of the abolition of women's pornographic magazines, and not men's, in the 2000s angered me at the time, fuelled by my enthusiasm for creating women's erotica in the 1990s. Today, if presented with the two options: pornographic magazines for all sexualities stocked or pornographic magazines unavailable in convenience stores, I would vote for the latter. The reason is clear. A few years ago, a woman who had gone on a domestic holiday with her baby had posted dejectedly on social media that she couldn't find nappies in convenience stores. For the first time, my eyes were opened in a shocking way: of course, the equivalent of men's erotica wasn't women's erotica—no, it was nappies for babies.

Japanese society is excessively well arranged to accommodate men's ejaculations. Individual rooms to watch pornographic DVDs are available for hire near most subway stations; sex is easily purchased on the internet; pornographic posters of two-dimensional girls are plastered all over Akihabara; and a multitude of posters advertise many and varied sex trade venues throughout the city. In this climate, when a victim of sexual violence speaks out, she is shouted down powerfully in the same way that feminists are. Convenience store pornographic magazines act like a supporting pillar of this structure. We women have so little that the situation can't possibly be balanced out simply by putting women's erotica on shelves alongside men's erotica.

There is no limit to the things which are so comprehensively absent for women, so we don't notice their absence: access to an affordable and timely morning-after pill, a trustworthy system for sexual abuse victims to speak up, safe abortions, financial security for women to have babies... Not long ago, a story about an infant being disposed of in a convenience store toilet was in the news, and it's not that difficult to imagine the circumstances in which a woman has to dispose of a new-born baby in Japan. A culture and industry catering to men's ejaculations is well established and normalised, whereas women's actual needs aren't being met. For women's sexuality, furthermore, there is absolutely nothing. The situation we are placed in is laughable in its desolation; it's hell.

As I was writing this article, the news came out that a TENGA[2] permanent stall will be set up in the men's section of the Hankyu department store in Osaka. We can see what the shop will be like from the photos in the news stories. And so, with motifs of rainbows and of love, and the tagline 'bringing sex to the high street', we have arrived at a point where department stores sell male masturbatory goods. Should I, with men, be happy at the arrival of this new sexual culture? Or should I be wary that it's another pitfall? Would be it ok if women's sex goods were also sold in department stores? But why do men's things always come first? How does the 'high street-ification' of men's ejaculatory goods interlink with the disappearance from convenience stores of pornographic magazines for men? I ponder these things as I wait for summer, when pornographic magazines will vanish from convenience store shelves. I hope that, when we look back, this year will be remembered as one in which we took one step towards making sexual discrimination history.

---

[2] A sex goods shop.

What follows is a translation of a speech given by Kitahara Minori on the occasion of the first 'Flower demo' event of 2021, which was held online on 11 January due to pandemic restrictions in Tokyo at the time. The other speakers were Ishida Ikuko, who, after pursuing years of court action against her own childhood attacker, leads campaigning efforts in Japan against teacher-perpetrated sexual abuse, and in support of law reform; Spring director, Yamamoto Jun (see Chapter 3); Ogawa Fumi, a suicide counsellor and social worker; writer Ogawa Tamako; Matsuo Akiko, chief editor of etc. books and Makino Masako, a sociologist who has researched the 'chikan' public sexual assault problem.

The First 'Flower demo' of 2021

Today's 'Flower demo' event is the first for 2021 and marks the second year of campaigning. Now we're in the second year, I'd like to reflect on that time, and reflect on why the 'Flower demo' campaign began. It began in April 2019 in response to a series of 4 sex crime acquittals. A father abused his daughter for many years and was found not guilty; sex with someone made to drink several tequilas until losing consciousness was found not to be a criminal act; a 12-year-old girl's testimony was found to have no grounds—despite acknowledging her inability to fight back—and her rapist found not guilty, because he might have misunderstood that she wasn't consenting. Many people spoke out about how wrong these acquittals were and called for gender education for court judges.

However, these calls were met with ridicule and cynicism, mainly from lawyers who said that a judge's decision should be respected. They said that lay people shouldn't be criticising these kinds of court decisions. We also heard people say that while #MeToo might be understandable, what about human rights? This was a sobering reminder that women's rights are not seen as human rights! Calling out questionable things isn't wrong; why were these verdicts passed down? We couldn't shake off these questions, and so got together on 11 April 2019.

The voices of sexual assault victims are not heard, and any voice resonating with their voices is scorned as too emotional. In the first place, women are not believed in this society. That despair and anger spurred us on, and more than 500 people gathered on that day. The event wasn't referred to as a 'Flower demo' at that point. The aim of getting everyone together was to spread the #MeToo and #WeToo messages, and we decided to bring flowers along to the event. It has long been said that Japan hasn't really had a #MeToo movement yet, and this is put down to a lack of consciousness on the part of women born and raised in this country. But this explanation is wrong. Sexual assault victims have been unable to speak out safely in this society where, when they try, they are ridiculed with a force that crushes them. This is a society that gives a platform to people who slander victims by questioning whether they had a vendetta against the man or were financially motivated. This is why we needed to take a #WithYou stance that showed empathy for victims and showed we believed them.

We chose the flower as a symbol of #WithYou. It's not that we want to be flowers, or that we want to be treated like flowers. The flowers are a message of hope for victims recovering from pain, and are a message of solidarity.[3] The stories that emerged from all those people gathered on 11 April were stories of individual suffering. Women who had been forced into silence for so long started talking. No witnesses, no evidence. They no longer wished to ignore the pain of being unable to forget something they had tried so hard and for so long to forget. We don't want to make the next generation go through the same thing. One by one, women started talking, driven by a desire to change society. The talking went on and on, and that day, I realised that it could not be contained in one event. This was the beginning.

After the first event, women from a number of different regions expressed a desire to hold their own events. Among these women were long-time anti-sexual violence activists as well as those who had never organised an event like this. There were many who said they wanted to stage an event even if it meant doing so alone. A lot of sexual violence occurs in places that should be the safest, like commuting to school or work, at work or at school, or inside the home. It is for this reason that the solidarity of the 'Flower demo' events has spread all over the country, to the amazement of the organisers themselves, who have been so determined to protest against sexual violence in their own cities.

As of March 2020, events are being held in all 47 Japanese prefectures, as well as in Barcelona. In the beginning, none of the organisers imagined

---

[3] In other forums, Kitahara has explained that the idea to use flowers as part of the events was inspired by the Seoul-based Marymond social enterprise business that supports 'comfort women' survivors. This business sells goods printed with flowers chosen by survivors.

the 'Flower demo' would be a place to discuss sexual violence. Even so, there was no end to the people who came to talk about their own pain. With each event, the #MeToo voices got louder as each story invited another one. As time passed, I once again thought about how sexual assault victims had been struggling on their own. They got sick, could no longer stomach food, and they tried a variety of ways to convey what was going on. But many of them were not believed. Some stopped trying, believing no one would understand. So they were forced into silence. It's not that victims weren't able to speak; it's that society wouldn't listen to them. It is for this reason that, through the 'Flower demo' events, we realised that this society needed the very space created by them for listening to and believing victims. I truly feel that the voices heard over the last 2 years are powerful in our society. The honesty of the victims is the strength that reveals the nature of sexual violence and has the ability to change society's indifference and bias. Also, their voices expose the violence that is inherent in the so-called neutral approach to judging sexual violence cases which involves listening to both sides of the story to see who is lying. Victims brought to light pain from living in a severely patriarchal culture where women's human rights are derided, diversity is not understood, and sex is commodified.

Ultimately, 3 out of the 4 acquittal verdicts that were the impetus for the creation of the 'Flower demo' events were overturned (prosecutors didn't appeal one of them) and perpetrators were found guilty, even with very little new evidence or information. Victims speaking about the reality of sexual violence has changed society's understanding of it. Speaking out is not in vain. I believe that embattled voices produced these verdicts of hope.

The so-called 'Flower demos' are events that oppose sexual discrimination, speak out to eradicate sexual violence, and call for social change. They are not centrally organised with a leader, but have developed through the independent leadership and solidarity of local organisers. There are regions where the protests are student-led, others where they are held by the LBGTQ community, others where they dance in protest, and still others that actively lobby politicians. There are also not a small number of regions that have become new spaces for long-time women's rights activists and young women to meet each other. Loosely connected via social media, and with organisers from cities across 47 prefectures, we are united by the desire to change this world, get rid of sexual violence, and call for change to the Penal Code from the perspective of sexual crime victims. I believe it is because we loosely accept each other's differences that we are so strongly unified and have been able to progress with unprecedented momentum.

It goes without saying that the issue of sexual violence has been continually taken up by the women's movement, which has a long history. The 'Flower demos' walk a path already paved by numerous women's movements and victim support groups. I refer to 'we' because I know that in a society that devalues women's voices, that devalues diversity of sexuality, and that treats sex as a commodity, our pain is individual and yet very similar. Speaking about our problems is speaking about society's problems. Women and children are even more vulnerable now in the pandemic and are being crushed. For this reason, to ensure that no victim suffering from patriarchy, misogyny, or gender inequality is left behind, I would like for us to continue to speak out as we, in solidarity with 'Flower demo' allies, consolidate our commitment to real social change.

CHAPTER 3

Yamamoto Jun: Survivor-Activist for the Sexually Abused

Abstract This chapter discusses developments continuing in Japan since 2014 to amend sex offence provisions in the country's penal code. These developments have been propelled by sexual abuse survivors, including the focus of the chapter: the founder of the organisation 'Spring', Yamamoto Jun. This organisation, and Yamamoto, have been central to changes in Japanese law that bring the country into better alignment with judicial systems that understand sexual abuse to be a crime attributable to perpetrators and not victims. The importance of lobbying politicians, and other tactics towards legislative change, are discussed in the chapter as is the importance, as mentioned also by Kitahara in the previous chapter, of public uprising over issues like sexual violence, which helped Yamamoto's campaigning for legislative change. The chapter emphasises pragmatism in campaigning, to set aside differences among those working together as allies towards a defined goal. The impact of Yamamoto's memoir, describing her hardship as a childhood incest survivor, is also noted as having been significant in influencing the Japanese public, and also a key politician.

Keywords Yamamoto Jun · Spring · Penal Code · Sex offences · 'Flower demo' · Legislative change · Lobbying of politicians · Survivor activism · Male-dominated society

© The Author(s), under exclusive license to Springer Nature Singapore Pte Ltd. 2022
E. Dalton and C. Norma, *Voices from the Contemporary Japanese Feminist Movement*, Palgrave Macmillan Studies on Human Rights in Asia, https://doi.org/10.1007/978-981-19-2228-2_3

In 2017, for the first time in 110 years, Japan's rape and sexual assault legislation was amended. The main amendments included lengthening prison sentences for perpetrators, incorporating males in the definition of victim, and creating a new crime addressing sexual abuse by guardians. Yamamoto Jun, as relayed in her discussion below, had campaigned with other activists for these amendments and others. They did not achieve an amendment that would remove the requirement for victims to prove force or intimidation to establish the crime of rape, nor was Japan's age-of-consent raised. Yamamoto and her colleagues did, however, succeed in getting these recommendations and others included as supplementary amendments that would be considered in three years' time. In 2020, Yamamoto was selected to serve on the advisory council that would review these recommended additional amendments.

The extent of Yamamoto's effectiveness as an activist in just a few years is shown to have been a feat of fortitude and bravery by the life she led up to it. Yamamoto was sexually abused by her father for 7 years from the age of 13. She was freed from his abuse when her parents split up, and she and her mother moved from Tokyo to Japan's west. She subsequently became a nurse and did not speak much of her experience to anyone other than counsellors. Her feminist hackles were raised, though, one by one, as she gradually began sorting through her trauma. She went to feminist counselling where she felt able to talk about things she could not talk about elsewhere. In 2005, at the age of 31, she began attending violence awareness courses for girls and women, not as a subject but as an observer, because she could not yet tell people about her abuse, and a part of her believed that what had happened to her was not worth making a fuss over. She attended these courses under the guise of her profession: she told organisers she wanted to learn about how to deal with patients who presented as victims of violence. This was not untrue, and eventually she specialised in this area, obtaining a master's degree in nursing from a university in Tokyo, and qualifying as a Sexual Assault Nurse Examiner.

An 8-day training seminar in Canada in 2007 had a profound impact on Yamamoto. She felt as though she had travelled 30 years into the future, so different and refreshing was the approach to sexual abuse compared to what she had seen in Japan. It was there that she came into contact with the concept of survivor-centred treatment and care; she was taken with the concept of 'survivor', and decided she liked the term for herself because she believed she was a survivor, not just of the abuse but of the ongoing effects of trauma.

Around this time, she began to meet activists and NGO workers involved in tackling sexual abuse. It was at age 36, in 2010, when Yamamoto finally felt able to face her trauma head on, and when she did so publicly, she became a spokesperson for abused children and women across Japan. In February 2017, Yamamoto published a candid account of how the abuse had affected her: *Jūsansai, 'Watashi' wo Nakushita Watashi* ('Losing Myself at Age 13'). The timing of the book coincided with Japan's Penal Code sex crimes amendments of the same year—something for which Yamamoto had lobbied as a member of a sexual abuse survivors' group.

The legislative origins of the 2017 amendments can be traced to a commission into sexual offence penalties set up by Japan's Ministry of Justice in 2014. This commission, which disbanded in August 2015, prompted the establishment in the same year of a deliberative council concerned with Penal Code sexual offences amendments. Yamamoto did not want to leave the deliberations to people who she believed were not aware of the realities of sexual abuse, so she organised with some other survivors to lobby the government for changes that would reflect their needs. One particular comment she read in a report by the above-mentioned commission into sexual offence penalties spurred her into action: one member of the commission had suggested that there were very rare cases where sexual relations between parent and child could be consensual (WAN Josei Kikin).

After the 2017 amendments, Yamamoto founded the organisation Spring, a sexual abuse survivor-centred advocacy group, whose main activity is lobbying the government to change the sex crime provisions. Spring has had remarkable success lobbying politicians all across the political spectrum. Its primary focus is on legislative change, so lobbying politicians from the ruling Liberal Democratic Party has been especially important. When Spring started lobbying in 2017, so strong was the stigma attached to talking about sexual abuse that Yamamoto was told by one Diet member to keep the fact of their meeting private (Yamamoto). Today, Spring's website is filled with photos of Yamamoto and her fellow activists posing with smiling politicians. It is no exaggeration to say that there has been a tectonic shift in the way that sexual assault and abuse is approached in Japan over the latter half of the 2010s. It has been a complex and ongoing shift with multi-layered causal factors, but Yamamoto and her supporters have been central contributors.

Yamamoto's driving aim, borne from personal experience, is to change the law for the benefit of sexual abuse victims.

Yamamoto stepped down from her director position at Spring in October 2021 to focus on her role in the advisory council on sex crimes within the Ministry of Justice. The authors in 2019 had attended Yamamoto's keynote speech at the Japan Association of Gender and Law conference at Osaka University titled, 'Rape myths and judicial fairness'. We interviewed Yamamoto in downtown Tokyo in July 2021.

Spring

I became involved in the Penal Code sex crimes amendments in 2015, when some others and I founded the group *Seibōryoku to Keihō wo Kangaeru Tōjisha no Kai* (Survivors concerned with sexual violence and the Penal Code). We were a group of around 5 people. We began lobbying the government for changes to the law and stepped up our efforts between autumn 2016 and June 2017, when we joined forces with 3 other organisations. We called for further amendments to be included in the Penal Code sex offences amendment bill that was submitted to the Diet in January 2017 that would, among other things, abolish the requirement for victims to prove force or intimidation, lift the age-of-consent, extend the statute of limitations, and newly include penalties for sexual violence perpetrated through someone taking advantage of a position of power. We knew that, in Japan, once the text of a bill has been created by the Ministry of Justice and submitted to the Diet, it isn't likely to be thereafter changed much, but even so, we wanted our requests reflected in the bill even just a little bit, so we lobbied MPs twice a month and spoke to a number of Diet members who told us that, even though the text of the bill probably wouldn't change, our opinions could go into a schedule of supplementary provisions and resolutions. So, in the end, when the law was amended in June 2017, the requirement for force or intimidation remained, but our suggestion that people working in the courts and the police force undergo training was added as a supplementary resolution, and a supplementary provision was added to the effect that the law would be considered for review in 3 years'time.

I had been working closely with Kamata Kanoko from the organisation Community Organizing Japan.[1] She had been lobbying with me from the start, back when some of the Diet members really didn't understand the issue at all. Over time we brought some of them around, and Kamata told me it would be a waste to not take advantage of the connections we had made. I was tired by this stage and wondered if I could do it all again, but because of the inclusion of the supplementary provisions that would be reviewed in 3 years, we realised we had to keep going, otherwise they might not go anywhere.

So, in June, I disbanded Survivors concerned with sexual violence and the Penal Code, and we reorganised as Spring on 7 July 2017. In effect, we changed from a volunteer organisation to a legal entity registered with the Legal Affairs Bureau. We formed as an organisation centred around victims, and then we became the first organisation in Japan to have incorporated as an association of sexual abuse victims.

The supplementary schedule to the 2017 amendment law requires not 'revision' but 'consideration of review', and in actual fact, there has been no review yet undertaken, even though we are now in 2021. But an advisory council was convened for this purpose in 2020, and I was selected to be on it on 30 March 2020. In the years in between, when the law was amended and the advisory council created, the Ministry of Justice set up a fact-finding working group to assess how things had been going since the legislative amendments.

SHIFTING SOCIAL AWARENESS LEADS TO POLICY CHANGE

Compared to before, we hear the voices of victims in Japan more loudly these days. When you think about how, before, those voices weren't reaching anyone at all in Japan, I think they are a little bit more audible now. Whether they are being properly reflected or not, though, I'm not sure.

In 2017, we didn't even know if there would be any legislative amendments, or whether a review would be considered in 3 years' time. The

---

[1] Community Organizing Japan is an NPO founded in 2013 that coaches grassroots organisations in Japan. Kamata, who co-founded the organisation, was trained in campaign organising at the Harvard Kennedy School. A victim of sexual assault herself, she and Community Organizing Japan helped Yamamoto establish Spring.

first thing that happened was that in December 2017, Liberal Democratic Party members of the Diet started a Diet member alliance. Its name is *Seibōryoku no Nai Shakai wo Tsukuru Giin Renmei* (Group to create a society without sexual violence), and the creation of this group, also known as the *Wan Tsū Giren* (One too alliance), was quite a big deal. The Alliance regularly submits written requests for updates on the legislative amendments and keeps working on the issue for us. The head of the Alliance is Kamikawa Yōko, a former minister of justice. The fact that she has shown concern and has been in our corner probably had a positive effect on our dealings with the Ministry. Spring lobbies the government once a month, and as a result, there are now Diet members who understand what we're doing. There has been a major change over the last 3 years: questions on the issue are now asked in the Diet. Previously, the issue of sexual violence and sex crimes was not raised in the Diet.

Then, in 2019, after a series of 4 sex crime acquittals, the 'Flower demo' events began in April. This was, I think, a result of a shift in public opinion. The effectiveness of the 'Flower demo' movement across the country—if we see it as one undertaken by people external to the judiciary and the Diet, people we might call 'outsiders'—was that the issue of sexual violence was made visible. For Japan, this was a major step forward. In the context of these social shifts, in 2020, the government published guidelines on strengthening anti-sexual violence measures.[2] This was the first time the state had really dealt with the issue as a priority, so I believe this was ground-breaking.

Raising awareness among the general public is important, but so is engaging individual politicians who will fight for the cause in the Diet. I think both are important. It's important to keep pushing Diet members as 'insiders', and also important as an outsider to raise awareness of the issue so it's more visible to members of the Diet who will then become interested in it as it affects their potential votes. But, still, regardless of how much public attention an issue attracts, just as with the neglect of the separate surnames bill,[3] there needs to be action taken by both

---

[2] *Sei Hanzai, Seibōryoku Taisaku no Kyōka no Hōshin*, see the Ministry of Justice website: https://www.gender.go.jp/policy/no_violence/seibouryoku/measures.html.

[3] Japan's Civil Code requires married couples to have the same surname. This has been something that some women's organisations have agitated over for decades. In 2021, the Supreme Court threw out, not for the first time, an appeal by a group of plaintiffs to overturn the Civil Code on the basis that the separate surname requirement violates

civil society as well as insiders. Otherwise, the Diet will, in the end, turn against the issue.

Three years ago, talking about sexual abuse was a big taboo, but then the #MeToo movement arose and Itō Shiori spoke out. Then the 'Flower demo' events began, so I think the issue is being taken up a fair bit now. Although, at the moment, the pandemic dominates most talk. In the media there are women journalists who have continuously raised the issue, thankfully. But even so, I've heard from journalists that even though Japan ranks really low in the Global Gender Gap Index, male bosses in local media stations resist running stories on the topic, saying things like, 'Now's not the time', or questioning their relevance even when women journalists enthusiastically back them.

As for the average person, they are, to some extent, now more exposed to the issues via things like the 'Flower demo'. Itō Shiori's impact was big enough that the average person knows about her. When she went public in 2017, she fell victim to an extreme backlash—well, second rape, really. Such was the climate: that someone who had their drink spiked and who was violated while at a work consultation was then punished for speaking up. In the past, that kind of incident would have been swept under the rug. But with Itō Shiori speaking out, and various movements rising up, now more people say, 'I don't think you can do it without consent'. But on the other hand, there are those who still say, 'In that case, then everything will be a crime'. There has been an increase in those believing the former over the latter. This has been a change in the last 3 years. Victims can speak more freely now. Before, victims of teachers or their own lovers would come under attack themselves if they spoke out.

Our activism has become easier too, thanks to the impact of things like the 'Flower demo' campaign, and people like Itō Shiori. It helps when famous people speak up, like the celebrity Shelly, and like Kojima Keiko, who have been discussing issues like these since 2017. When people like that push from the outside and influence public opinion, it makes it easier for Spring's lobbying activities.

---

principles of equality and was therefore unconstitutional. A bill to revise this system was drafted as far back as 1996, but the ruling Liberal Democratic Party's dogged opposition to revision, even in the face of public support of a separate surname system, has stymied the introduction of that bill or anything similar for debate in the Diet, where, the Supreme Court said, the issue needs to be solved (Siripala).

I think when an issue gains public interest, this leads to Diet members becoming interested too. If the public gets behind an issue and takes something on though, and it doesn't end up being reflected in practical policy—say, like the bill to revise the Penal Code, or in support measures for victims—then people feel like there's nowhere to go from there. Complaints and frustration without change lead to disappointment that weakens the movement. With this in mind, Spring was the organisation that led the charge for Penal Code reform, and pursued a specific goal, and made progress towards that goal. I think we've made good progress. Opposition to nuclear power was a huge movement, but ultimately nothing changed. It's important for changes to happen while there is momentum. The nuclear power issue is very difficult because of so many competing interests. It's important to get results.

Still a Long Way to Go: The Root of the Problem

The gender unequal situation in Japan is not right. And now, because of the pandemic, we have the 'women's recession', and female suicide rates have increased hugely too. I think the fact that women are forced into low-paid, short-term and non-regular jobs, like those in hotels or hospitality reflects the gender gap. The wage of a male regular worker is 3 or 4 times that of a female non-regular worker. In this scenario, women will naturally be harder hit in a recession, given the type of capitalism we have, but also, they get sexually harassed because of their vulnerable position. Then there's poverty, and sexual and maternity harassment pushes women out of jobs so they become even poorer. It's this endless vicious cycle that I believe produces a society where women and men can't work equally, and under these circumstances, sexual violence can't be solved. We have to move forward understanding this.

I think gender inequality is at the root of sexual violence. There's this idea that men can do whatever they like to women, and when women find themselves in such a situation (and children too), the general public thinks it's normal and so doesn't respond when a woman speaks up about being sexually harassed. In this context, women have no choice but to give up because society does nothing for them. They are led to believe that they're the ones in the wrong. I think the message needs to be clear that it doesn't matter who it is, sexual violence isn't acceptable. A huge problem is that men and women see things very differently. A man might think that he is, in his own way, being a good guy, but under the surface, things are completely different.

As for the relationship between sexual violence and women's difficulty securing financial independence, there is the pay gap, but it's also difficult to work as a fulltime regular worker when you're forced to take on housework and childcare because of the gendered division of labour. I believe this might be a problem around the world. There is also the fact that there aren't enough childcare places, and men can't commit to childcare or housework because of their long work hours. The result is that housework and childcare become women's role and are seen as inevitable: if women can't work consistently long hours, the fact they get low wages and are non-regular workers can't be helped. In this way, their social position drops, and they become more vulnerable to disadvantage.

I think one of the things keeping Japan from achieving gender equality is that there's a mismatch between men's and women's perceptions. Women consider people's feelings, while men don't realise when they've misunderstood things, even when their intentions might have been good. I think this is the case even in legal debates and in the Ministry of Justice advisory council on sex crimes. Men can only imagine situations through men's eyes, with men's bodies. Most sex crime victims are women, so I think that men aren't really able to imagine how a woman experiences victimisation; for example, why women freeze and can't vocalise anything when they're attacked. Men and boys can have the same reactions, but the fact we live in a male-dominated society comes into play. The debates lack a wide range of values. For change to happen, a wider range of people from diverse backgrounds needs to replace the older men in politics. Unfortunately, until now, a lot of relatively unthinking voters have preferred the status quo. But I think a lot of voters are suffering at the moment; they're in trouble, and maybe it's become a bit easier for people to speak out. Childcare is a good example—lots of people are speaking out about the need for more childcare these days and this is new. People need to start electing politicians who look like they will implement the things they want.

I do think it's a little bit easier now for women to speak up about sexual abuse. For example, anti-sexual harassment guidelines have been created, and there are calls to turn them into law so that all companies have to comply. But small-to-medium companies, especially those that are struggling, might find it difficult to comply because they might want to retain those men who generate them profits.

Working with Politicians: The Pragmatic Feminist Approach

In terms of other groups that we cooperate with, there's the umbrella group *Keihō Kaisei Shimin Purojekuto* (Penal Code amendment citizens' project) which incorporates 12 organisations, and there's the human trafficking organisation Lighthouse, and Voice Up Japan, which is what you would probably call an 'outsider' group and not one centrally involved with Penal Code amendments. In terms of cooperation from the government, the LDP *Wan Tsū Giren* (One too alliance) has been good. The name of the organisation comes from the White House movement '1 is 2 Many', which was launched on the basis that even one victim of sexual violence is too many, and so sexual violence must be eradicated.

In April 2017, I met Akazawa Ryōsei, a member of the committee of judicial affairs and vice chair of the Liberal Democratic Party Diet policy committee, and gave him my book *Losing Myself at Age 13*, to convey to him the essence of what we were asking for in requesting amendments to the Penal Code. Reading my book was a light bulb moment for him and he decided that, as a human being, he couldn't tolerate sexual violence, so he said he would act. It was thanks to him that the supplementary resolution was appended to the legislative amendment in the way we proposed. Now there are several Diet members committed to the cause—in the opposition parties as well—but still, it was Diet member Akawaza who worked with us to make sure it was done properly.

The ruling party has the power to change things. I don't know if things will change with the upcoming election, but it doesn't look like the Constitutional Democratic Party of Japan will take power. Which political party we have to deal with doesn't really matter to us; we don't really have a preference. We would like to see change to the Penal Code, and we would like to see justice done.

The 5 or 6 other organisations that have collaborated with and supported us for a long time are not that interested in politics. Spring really just has a mission to get our demands met. But some of the other organisations were a bit pickier and preferred talking to opposition party Diet members. To be sure, the opposition party female Diet members are really open, and some, but not all, of the opposition party men are too. But regardless of who you're talking to, you don't go and see the person you want to see, you see the person who will see you and who will change things. That's Spring's approach.

I'm also involved with *Shiawase Namida* (Happy tears), which is an organisation concerned with the sexual abuse of people with disabilities. I'm close to the director, Nakano Hiromi, who was also a board member at Spring, and I've worked with her for many years. I wasn't really involved in any other type of activism before this. I mean, I've always been opposed to nuclear power, but the coalition parties are pro-nuclear. And it's a bit difficult to take an anti-government stance. If we split over the issue of nuclear power, I won't be able to work with them as the director of Spring, right? As an individual I probably could, but it becomes a question of balance.

There is a citizens' project that surveys members of the Diet about their interest in the issue of sexual violence and their desire to change things. The plan is to publicise the results and to encourage people to elect those committed to tackling sexual abuse in the next election, and to vote out those who are not. I think this kind of approach will bring about change. I believe it's important to vote the right people in; to make sure people in the world of politics are thinking about people. I do believe that if people are engaged things will change. Before I started lobbying, I had never spoken to a politician, not until about 2016. I had no idea about how to meet them or what to talk about, but when they did meet to talk, I got my message across and saw that things can change. I realised that voting is important; I wished that everyone would get engaged in lobbying. It's difficult, but I believe that if there is something you want to change, lobbying is effective.

When I talk about feminism, what I mean is: within a male-centred society that was created by men, the question of how those who aren't men should live their lives, or how to create a society that isn't male-centred, hasn't really been pursued. I believe feminism is the pursuit of questions about how we, regardless of sex or race, can live equally, while respecting each other's rights. But there are too many different types of feminisms and this can be tiring. Maybe people think differently. We have to reach a point where people who have been oppressed—people whose voices have been silenced—learn to value themselves, and others recognise their value as well.

CHAPTER 4

Nitō Yumeno: Collaborating for the Rights of Teenage Girls

Abstract The influence exercised by Nitō Yumeno and her organisation Colabo is discussed in this chapter as an extraordinary example of feminist activism achieving significant results in Japan. The chapter suggests that, largely thanks to Nitō's efforts via Colabo, the 1990s' mischaracterisation of child prostitution in Japan as 'compensated dating' is now largely dispelled, and progressive efforts against the sex industry, and particularly its abuse of young homeless women, are substantially underway in the second decade of the twenty-first century. The chapter first describes Nitō's personal growth as a feminist in reaction to hostility and harassment after stepping forward in support of exploited women, and her concern that the only people who reach out to troubled teens are men seeking to abuse or exploit them. The chapter canvasses serious problems in Japan's public welfare infrastructure as it responds to children, and reflects upon adjustments Colabo has had to make in the pandemic to better cater to vulnerable young women in Tokyo's entertainment districts. Nitō urges assistance from adults who she wishes would intervene in the rampant scouting and soliciting of young women on Tokyo's streets. The chapter lastly conveys Nitō's view that prostitution buyers should be penalised in measures against the sex trade in Japan.

© The Author(s), under exclusive license to Springer Nature Singapore Pte Ltd. 2022
E. Dalton and C. Norma, *Voices from the Contemporary Japanese Feminist Movement*, Palgrave Macmillan Studies on Human Rights in Asia, https://doi.org/10.1007/978-981-19-2228-2_4

Keywords Nito Yumeno · Colabo · Child prostitution · 'Compensated dating' · Youth welfare services · 'Self-help' mentality in Japan · Tsubomi night cafe

Nitō Yumeno, born in 1989, launched a Tokyo-based NGO called Colabo in 2017, which has as its mission to 'create a society in which all girls have clothing, food, shelter and people they can rely on…in which girls in trouble do not find themselves being exploited or exposed to violence' (https://colabo-official.net/projects-english/). The organisation undertakes outreach work among teenage girls in inner-city Tokyo where throngs of vulnerable young women end up on the streets of its entertainment districts after fleeing abusive households, being lured from regional areas by 'scouts' posing as boyfriends, or after finding themselves desperate for money after exploitation and betrayal in the mainstream labour market (see Fujita).

While Colabo is a direct-service organisation, and receives local government funding as well as widespread public support in the form of donations for its concrete assistance offered vulnerable girls, Nitō's leadership has made the organisation concurrently one of considerable political influence in Japan. Her strong public speaking skills, networking techniques, and ability to convey sophisticated analyses of social problems, sees her appearing regularly on the Tokyo Broadcasting System weekly program 'Sunday Morning', occupying a seat on the Tokyo Metropolitan government youth problems commission, as well as acting as a consultant to a Ministry of Health, Labour and Welfare committee to address female disadvantage. The arguments that Nitō pursues through these venues about the responsibility of adults to create a social environment in which men do not sexually prey upon girls made homeless through abuse and violence have only become more persuasive over the years of the pandemic.

Under Nitō's leadership, Colabo has grown exponentially over 5 years, and some of this success is attributable to the *Watashi wa Kawareta* ('I Was Bought') travelling photo exhibition that Nitō curated with young women formerly assisted by Colabo, who describe their experiences of hardship in Japan's sex industry. As Nitō mentions below, this exhibition is still held in various venues around Japan, and operates both as a fundraising and public education initiative to combat the harms of prostitution for girls. Colabo has been the focus of a number of television documentaries that have reported on the exhibition, and Japan's mainstream newspapers regularly cover the organisation's other activities. Less known in mainstream circles is an innovative web-based video project produced by Nitō in collaboration with two young women (now working with Colabo as former beneficiaries of assistance). In the series, the young women describe their own experiences, as well as those of other women assisted by Colabo, in encountering *'kimoi ojisan'* ('sleezy guys'). That is, the video series relays personal testimony lodged by young women subjected to sexual harassment, public molestation, attempts at procurement and solicitation for prostitution and the like, which are forms of violence that apparently comprise a backdrop to the lives of girls on the streets of inner-city Tokyo. The video discussions between the women appear light-hearted and fun, as the title of the program indicates, but at the same time comprise an extraordinary record of the nature, variety, and extent of the predatory sexual behaviour that men in Japan exercise against the country's young women.

Nitō has published 2 non-fiction books, which have also significantly contributed to public awareness of Colabo and its activities. The first was published in 2013 (with a second edition published in 2015), just after Colabo was officially registered as an NGO in March 2013. The book describes Nitō's own life as a teenage high-school drop-out, and personal experiences in a Tokyo inner-city entertainment district, before receiving help from an organisation promoting school re-entry through farm stays and independently run classes. Nitō's extraordinary life story told in this publication, titled, *Nanmin Kōkōsei: Zetsubō Shakai wo Ikinuku Watashitachi no Riaru* (Refugee schoolgirls: our lives overcoming a society of despair), reflects her personal determination to overcome an abusive, neglectful household to personally succeed, but also to help women in Japan's sex industry who were not similarly fortunate. The assistance that Nitō received meant she was able to graduate from Meiji University at age 23, and subsequently lead a major fundraising project in an area hit by the 2011 earthquake disaster. This project involved collaboration with local high-school girls to create a locally produced food product that generated significant sales. It was this successful initiative that prompted Colabo's later creation and prefaced its focus on teenage girls facing disadvantage and hardship. In the case of girls in Japan's inner-city entertainment districts, these hardships are described in Nitō's second book, published in 2014, titled *Joshi Kōsei no Ura Shakai* (The underground society of high-school girls). In this book, similar to the 'I Was Bought' exhibition, the lives of teenage girls on the streets and in 'entertainment' and sex industry venues are described from their own perspectives.

From Colabo's outset, Nitō has argued—drawing on her own experience of her high-school days—that the only people who reach out to the vulnerable and homeless teenage girls who are found in large numbers on the streets of inner-city Tokyo are men who are either aiming to prostitute them or pimp them. Specifically, in Nitō's words published in 2021:

> On any given night in the entertainment districts of either Shibuya or Shinjuku in downtown Tokyo, you will find hundreds of 'scout' pimps and sex buyers trawling the streets and approaching the teenage girls they find there. These men are adept at finding girls who are in trouble, and knowing what to say to them in order to get their trust. They approach the girls as if they're on their side. The 'scout' pimps ask if they've eaten, and tell the girls they'll be picked up by police if they hang around the streets, and so they should stay overnight with them instead. They tell the girls they can get them work, and offer them food and accommodation. But these are all means to sexual exploitation. These men are not offering the girls a social safety net, they are treating them as sex objects, consumables, and things to exploit. They are human traffickers. (Gōdō Shuppan 41)

In her discussion below, Nitō mentions the case of a girl effectively bought for the price of a rice-ball, when a man offered her a place to stay after finding her on the street in the cold because of having fled a violent father. The man immediately raped the girl upon leading her back to his house, which he did after buying her a rice-ball at a local convenience store. The girl had not had any prior sexual experiences. She later came under Colabo's care, and told her story as part of the travelling exhibition (Nitō, 'Gyakutai, Hinkon, Seibōryoku: Yoru No Machi Wo Samyou Shōjo Wo Sasaeru Mitsu No Katsudō'). Nitō also described her case in a media piece published in 2017. Her story, and the travelling exhibition, in the second decade of the twenty-first century, became an important counter-narrative to the propaganda that had dominated Japanese public discourse since the 1990s in which underage girls bought for prostitution by men under a guise of 'compensated dating' were imagined to be petulant recipients of luxury goods and easy money. This defence of child prostitution was, extraordinarily, promoted even by feminist academic Chizuko Ueno (see, for example, Ueno), and served for many decades to discourage public action against the industry that had proliferated by the turn of the century to trade underage girls to men. While earlier established organisations, like People Against Prostitution and Sexual Violence (PAPS) and Lighthouse, had some role in the public education that contradicted this stereotyped view in the second decade of the twenty-first century, it was Nitō's efforts via Colabo that ultimately overturned left-leaning, 'progressive' defences of child prostitution in Japan, which are, these days, heard only rarely.

The first author first met Nitō in August 2019 at a lecture given by Morita Seiya of the Anti-Prostitution and Pornography Research Group (APP) held at Rikkyo University discussing counter-arguments to 'sex work' endorsements of prostitution as a form of 'work' and consumer activity. The second author met Nitō around the same time at a closed event that was organised as a networking opportunity for activists and survivors invited from South Korea to meet survivor counterparts affiliated with Colabo, as well as those affiliated with the above-mentioned PAPS.

Anti-prostitution activists and survivors in South Korea organised more than a decade ago (see this book's Conclusion), and now have a significant organisational and political base in the country, which makes them a sought-after group of feminists, in terms of exchange of knowledge and experience, for Japanese activists. Japan-based survivors and their support organisations, including Colabo, regularly hold events and joint projects with South Korean organisations like Salim Center, and Colabo members have, since 2019, both travelled to South Korea as well as sponsored the travel to Japan of sisters from the country. Nitō's discussion below, recorded on 25 September 2021, reflects the depth and breadth of Nitō's five-year immersion in one of Japan's most serious human rights fields, as an activist, public figure, social worker, and feminist.

Feminist Self-Awareness in Response to Backlash

My organisation Colabo supports teenage girls who are victims of sexual violence. It was through being maligned by people who didn't like my work with Colabo in this respect that I realised I was a feminist. They said insulting things like, 'Look, here comes a new feminist'. So I asked myself, 'Am I a feminist?', and realised that I was. People who speak out are vehemently attacked, and the same thing happened when I spoke up about the 'comfort women' issue. Ironically though, these attacks at least taught me that I was a feminist.

We have endured a lot of attacks on Twitter, especially in reaction to our 'I Was Bought' exhibition, which conveys the reality of child prostitution. We staged this exhibition in Sendai in September 2021, after a long break due to the pandemic. The angry voices escalate when you do activism that protests something. I think the goal of these people, who are afraid of the truth that we speak, is to muzzle us. So, I think, to some extent, the attacks on us are proof that our activism is effective, and so we shouldn't bow to them. Instead, Colabo will continue our activism and speaking up.

I did what I thought was necessary based on my own experiences, and I had no idea I would attract so much criticism for this activism from men and right-wing troll types—it has surprised me. But the more I get attacked, the more I feel they're threatened by me, because they want to trample on women's rights.

Feminism wasn't on my mind at all when I started my activism, but when I think about what I have done it was certainly feminist. You know, I was a high-school drop-out. My homelife was difficult and I didn't feel secure there. At the time, I was spending all my time in the city district, so I ended up just dropping out of school. But the school I went to was a Christian girls' school—I didn't like it at the time, and I have lots of bad memories of it—but it placed a lot of importance on female independence. Perhaps my schooling had something to do with my growing up to be a feminist.

CHILD PROSTITUTION

When I started this activism in 2011, I was a university student. But before then, in around 2005 or 2006, I was a school student, and my days were spent not wanting to go home because my home environment wasn't safe. Looking back now, I see what was happening to me at the time was probably abuse, and my father's behaviour towards my mother was probably domestic violence, but at the time I didn't see it like that because at that stage, no one had taught me what child abuse, human rights violations, or violence actually were. Instead, I thought I was wrong for feeling like I didn't want to go home. Because I didn't feel safe at home, I didn't want to go back home after school, so in the beginning, I took to grabbing something to eat at convenience stores and then hanging around on some steps somewhere. This escalated to not going home at all and wandering the streets of Shibuya most nights of the week.

The people who approached me when I was out like this weren't people who wanted to help; they were people who would put me in danger: sex industry pimps and sex buyers. They were the only ones who approached me, and I began to believe that my only worth was found in this kind of environment. I was 15 years old. Just standing in front of the bookshop *Tsutaya* in Shibuya, near the scramble crossing, even if you're in a school uniform, you'll get men in suits at all hours of the day and night asking, 'How much?' The term *enjo kōsai* appeared in the 1990s.[1] I have a problem with this term—I mean, how is it 'assistance'? Surely it's only in Japan that issues of child prostitution and the sexual exploitation of children are spoken about using a term like this—a term that implies an adult is helping out a child. It's a relationship of power and violence, not one of equality, which is what the word 'dating' suggests. It's a term created from a male perspective, and even I had internalised it and was made to think that girls were responsible for their own actions. I think the mindset that, 'It's the girl's responsibility; she does it because she likes it' is deeply engrained in this society. I mean, when I myself was a teenager, it was only those kinds of men, or pimps, who approached me, and I thought that was my only value in this society. Japanese society today places a high sexual value on high-school girls, and it was only later that I realised how wrong this was. But back then, I was made to believe that I had to capitalise on my youthful worth, and when you're scouted by those men you feel really happy to be appreciated. It was only those men who showed any interest, and they were the only ones who approached me.

Homelife Vulnerability

By contrast, at school I was getting into trouble. I was sleeping in class because I was having a hard time at home. Perhaps people have an image of what being safe at home looks like: they sit quietly on their sofas after a long day. Having an unsafe home life means being unable to do that. On the contrary, you are fearful, you think someone might come in anytime,

---

[1] Referred to problematically as 'compensated dating' in English.

and you jump at the sound of footsteps. For me, I was really nervous about using shared spaces in the household, so I timed my trips to the toilet and bathroom and when I brushed my teeth, to avoid other family members. Being careful about every little thing—you know, 'What can I eat that's in the refrigerator?'—makes for a stressful life in which you don't sleep well.

As a result, I was late for school more and more, and would sleep during class, and, as a result, got into trouble with the teachers. I was thought of as a naughty child, and at school we were told we should respect our parents. I felt bad that I wasn't living up to my parents' expectations. My mum developed depression, and my parents got divorced. During this process I came to mimic my father's criticisms of my mother as a failed parent because she would be unable to get out of bed or make meals—I myself agreed with dad. But Mum would sob uncontrollably during her unstable times, and there were moments I thought she might hit me over something very minor. Instead, she would cry and cuddle me, and I remember always wondering, 'Which Mum do I trust?', and being terribly scared. On the days Mum couldn't go into work, I'd come home from school wondering, 'Which Mum will it be today?'

That kind of thing made me not want to be at home. Abusive parents aren't always bad; they have their 'nice' days. In fact, I would feel such happiness and enormous gratitude to Mum when she made my school lunch. I'm often told, 'That's normal for mothers!', and yes, this would have been normal if it had been a daily occurrence. But it wasn't—on the contrary, school lunches were like a weight on me. Just thinking about my mother trying her best to make them when she was depressed, feelings of gratitude would bubble up inside me even though she had treated me badly. In fact, the people looking out for depressed mothers are their daughters, who think, 'Somehow I have to help her'.

And so, even if you want to distance yourself from an abusive parent, you can't, and it becomes a sort of co-dependence. Sure, there are people who ought to be arrested and locked up, and people are so keen to do this to abusive parents, but there are also parents who don't necessarily deserve this who are themselves in pain. Also, single parenting is impossible for some people. I believe that those sorts of parents need to be supported. I started my activism based on my own experiences because I wanted to create a society where teenage girls who have unstable home lives, or who are abused or impoverished, don't inevitably end up being victims of violence or sexual exploitation, but instead have lots of choices available to them.

Inadequate Welfare Services for Abused Girls

I really feel that welfare services for abused children aren't functioning in Japan. During my own time of abuse, I didn't think what was happening to me was abuse, and so I didn't think to contact any child protection services (*jidō sōdanjo*) because I had given up on adults. But things have changed, and lots of the girls I meet through Colabo have sought help, whether it be calling the number on the SOS cards that are handed out at schools, or through directly contacting a centre.

The junior high-school girl at the centre of the *onigiri* rice-ball episode had contacted a child protection services many times, and the centre had taken her into their care. But guardians often violate the human rights of children quite seriously. For instance, girls in custody can be kept out of school, they also have to strip down for full body checks, and their belongings are looked through. The child protection services say they do this to look for bruises. A few years ago, I went overseas to attend an international conference on welfare protection shelters. It was the first time for the conference to be held in Asia. Somebody talked about female university student protestors in Hong Kong being strip searched before being detained. Women participants from all over the world raised the fact that this was sexual violence. I hesitated to add my voice to the appeal—how could I when in Japan the same thing happens to protected children, to say nothing of those under arrest!

Girls with pierced ears have to remove their earrings before being taken into protection facilities in Japan. Some girls stay for as long as 1 or 2 months, or even a year or more, so the holes close, right? Which is not nice. And they can't take their own clothes with them; of course, they can't use their mobile phones, and sometimes they can't even attend school. So, it's one thing to tell children to contact the child protection services if they're abused, but these facilities don't always respond appropriately, and often a girl won't stay and will then be blamed for leaving of her own volition. But if they were places where girls wanted to stay, they wouldn't want to escape.

Some girls even say they will never contact a child protection services because their rules are too strict. The *onigiri* rice-ball girl was in her third year of junior high school when she came to us. All I did was ask if she'd contacted a centre, and then she ran off straight away, thinking that I was one of 'them'. This girl had been sitting on a step somewhere, unable to go home, when she was approached by a man who asked her what she was doing. After she told him about her situation, he bought her an *onigiri* rice-ball at the convenience store. He then took her by the hand and led her back to his home and raped her. We told her story in our 'I Was Bought' exhibition. The administration and underlying belief system of child welfare in Japan—the system and the thinking of the country itself (and this is true of social welfare in general)—is based on an understanding of welfare as a favour to its recipients. 'Self-help' is always the default. I started Colabo with no money, thinking that these children needed help, but even as recently as 2018 when I went to the city hall office, I was told by a Tokyo Metropolitan Assembly member that they should first help themselves (*jijo doryoku*).

There are abused girls who can't tell anyone they need help, and they come to us. They have nowhere to go for help, and, when they do seek help from welfare facilities, they're looked down upon, just like they're looked down upon by their schools. What's more, if you call a child protection services in the middle of night, you get an annoyed response. The government says that if you call the child abuse hotline it will be answered 24 hours a day, but actually it really depends a lot on the administrator as to who answers the phone—it might be a casual phone operator or a security guard who can't answer any questions and tells the caller to try again on Monday. Having a child protection services with a 24-hour phone service is vital. This isn't the reality at the moment, so when I meet girls in the middle of the night who need protection and I call the child protection services, the call gets redirected to the mobile of some poor staff member who I wake up.

Rise in Vulnerable Girls During the Pandemic

Colabo holds its 'Tsubomi night café' on Wednesday nights, around 3 times a month, in Kabukicho in downtown Tokyo. When a girl is being sexually exploited in the nightlife district, she is not in a position to seek help, and besides, there is no one out there who will help her. A helpdesk, like the ones attached to welfare facilities, is of no use to these girls. What's more, those places are open only during the day. So instead, we created a night-time space in the district where the girls actually are, so they can drop in easily. Our goal when we started in October 2018 was not to provide advice or consultation; instead, we just get to know the girls and let them know they can get meals from us. If they come to us for a meal we will chat and they might tell us about their problems, such as pregnancy or health issues. We give them our social media details, and then keep in touch with them to create a close relationship.

Our café has become really hectic since the pandemic because girls are in troubled and impoverished circumstances. In the 2019 financial year we had 590 people visit, but in 2020 the number was nearly 1500. This year it might even be higher. We set up the bus café so that girls engaged in nightlife district activities had a place to come for food and clothing, a chat, or to talk to someone about their problems. But actually, now, it's not just the girls in Kabukicho who turn up—there are lots of others who come to ask for help because there's nowhere else to go. We get 50 to 60 visitors every night—they're forming queues before the bus opens.

Originally, we had the bus open from 6 to 10 at night for the girls who were caught up in sexual exploitation in Kabukicho, because they normally go to work after 8 pm or 9 pm, so they'd come to us beforehand and grab something. But the extra 1000 who came through weren't those girls; they were people suffering in the pandemic, who in some way had the capacity to ask for help. Certainly, those girls are in a lot of trouble and, in fact, if we don't help them to find somewhere to stay, they too will soon be drawn into the sex trade. So, of course we've done what we can, because we have to help them. But what's happened is that, in 2020, our resources were overwhelmed in helping those who had the capacity to ask for help, and as a result, we weren't able to reach out to those girls who were stuck in situations that didn't allow them to seek help, those who had given up, those stuck in the sex trade, or those who have been made to believe they are to blame for their own situations. I look back on 2020 and regret this.

The bus is a really important place for those 50 or so people who turn up each time, and it would be good to have more places like that, in addition to Colabo. In 2020, the girls who turned up early to the bus café tended to snag the good things and the good places first, and so the atmosphere changed a little bit—the girls turning up later weren't as comfortable as they might have been. I wanted to ensure the bus was being used for its original mission, which was to help those girls who were not in a position to seek help (rather than girls who were in situations where they could), so from August this year, we changed the operating times to run from midnight, when the trains stop running, until 5 am.

This is the timeframe when girls are in the most trouble, when they can't get home. I knew this all along, but I didn't have the people power or finances to cope. The pandemic forced our hand, and now we're open on Wednesday nights from midnight until morning.

Where Are the Responsible Adults?

Bystander men turn a blind eye and don't say anything to the sex buyers, and to me this feels like a strange kind of male alliance. Instead of turning a blind eye, I wish there were more people who would say something to the pimps and sex buyers, like, 'What are you doing?' In our activist unit we have a team that goes out to the streets to talk to girls as well as an outreach team that works at the bus. The team on the streets has never once seen another person intervening in a sex buyer approaching a girl.

Our mission isn't to get girls to change; actually, I truly hope that girls can live however they want to live. It's adults who need to change. The fact that they don't is a real problem. There are so many men who believe that letting someone stay in their home and having sex with them is helping. They pretend to want to help girls, and approach them as though that's their purpose. When I read the girls' text message exchanges with the sex buyers, I can see that's how they frame it—as though they want to help the girls. They put a lot of work into seeking out and making connections with girls who are in no position to ask for help.

I think it's the right of girls to ask for help and it's the responsibility of adults to help them. I've worked with good supporters who do their best in a climate where they're just getting by with minimal funding for welfare activities, and when you're struggling like that, it's easy to get frustrated and think, 'But we're already giving you so much welfare'. But it's the responsibility of adults to provide welfare that ensures children have somewhere safe to live and sleep. Welfare, such as support from child protection services or social welfare facilities, aren't benefits—they are a guarantee of rights. But there's this mood—especially since the pandemic—of 'Let's all endure this together', which I think should be replaced with the sentiment, 'Let's not endure, but speak up'.

There really aren't any legal mechanisms in place in Japan to support young girls. Just today, there was a meeting in Tokyo of women consultants from local governments to talk about their assistance projects for young women. I attended to represent Colabo, but there were quite a few local governments who could cite no initiatives. I heard them talking about how they didn't know how to respond when teenage girls came asking for advice, and it made me realise how little support has been available until now. The very term for 'prostitution' in Japanese (*baishun*) is discriminatory. In Japan, it's the woman who 'sells' who is punished, when in reality, women are bought. The law turns the man into a passive being, as if the crime of prostitution is a woman's doing. Actually, at Colabo, we have been encouraged by the police to keep up our good work because the only thing they can do is arrest women in prostitution and take them into custody. I tell them that it shouldn't be like this, and that they should be doing something with the buyers. But they tell me that for this to happen, the law needs to change. Each individual citizen needs to become aware of this situation and speak out with others who are also concerned.

CHAPTER 5

Tsunoda Yukiko: Feminist Activist Lawyer

Abstract This chapter discusses the history of an early rape crisis center in Japan, and its role in eventually facilitating the recognition of sexual harassment as a civilly actionable claim in the country. Crucial to this history was feminist activist lawyer Tsunoda Yukiko whose testimony contributes most of the chapter's discussion. Tsunoda led Japan's first successful sexual harassment claim in court, and went on to represent many similar victims, as well as contribute to many feminist organisations, including Kibōtane and the Anti-Pornography and Prostitution Research Group. The chapter recalls the progression of sexual harassment as a recognised form of sex discrimination in Japan, which closely tracks the history of Tsunoda's legal career, which included a year's study abroad with Catharine MacKinnon at the University of Michigan. The chapter includes Tsunoda's reflections on improvements in the gender perspective of Japan's mass media, and her hope that feminists will take advantage of the opportunity raised by the International Labour Organization's recent requirement that member countries enact legal provisions against sexual harassment.

Keywords Tsunoda Yukiko · Sexual harassment law reform · Tokyo Rape Crisis Center · Catharine MacKinnon · Article 709 of Japan's Civil Code · Sexual harassment · Sex discrimination · International Labour Organization

© The Author(s), under exclusive license to Springer Nature Singapore Pte Ltd. 2022
E. Dalton and C. Norma, *Voices from the Contemporary Japanese Feminist Movement*, Palgrave Macmillan Studies on Human Rights in Asia, https://doi.org/10.1007/978-981-19-2228-2_5

We interviewed Tsunoda Yukiko on 21 June 2021 in the Kasumigaseki Law Offices building in Tokyo. Tsunoda had travelled that day on the bullet train to Tokyo from her home in Numazu for another meeting, and generously gave us 2 hours later in the day. The second author met Tsunoda for the first time in 2013 at Meiji University at a seminar on gender and constitutional law, and was thereafter in touch intermittently through the *Poruno Kaishun Mondai Kenkyū Kai* (Anti-Pornography and Prostitution Research Group), which Tsunoda had joined in 1999. From 2004 to 2013, Tsunoda taught a 'Gender and the law' subject in the graduate law school of Meiji University. Both authors saw her give a keynote speech titled 'Sexual victimisation and judicial gender bias: Analysis of criminal law judgements' at the 17th conference of the Japan Association of Gender and Law at Osaka University in November 2019. Even before this, both authors had read her 1991 book, which Tsunoda mentions in her discussion below (*Sei to Hōritsugaku*). They were therefore fascinated to hear how her ideas had developed on the topic of violence against women in the subsequent 30 years.

Tsunoda was born in 1942 in notoriously patriarchal Kitakyūshū, and was 77 years old at the time she spoke with the authors. In terms of both place of birth and age, Tsunoda defies expectations: her perspective is more radically feminist than other prominent members of Japan's contemporary women's movement, and her involvement in grassroots feminist activism seems more extensive now than even the earlier periods she describes of her life (her intensive legal work on behalf of women prior to retirement notwithstanding). For example, as she mentions below, Tsunoda in 2020 was involved with efforts for reform of the sex offence provisions of Japan's criminal code, 'Flower demo' events (see Tsunoda, 'Atarashii Yoake Wo Tsugeru Furawādemo'), *Kibōtane* (see https://www.kibotane.org/our-mission), and in campaigning for legal recognition of sexual harassment together with Itō Kazuko (see Tsunoda and Itō).

Tsunoda's feminist perspective developed after entering university, and upon joining a group called *Fujin Mondai Kenkyūkai* (Women's problems study group). The area she had grown up in, in Kitakyūshū, featured coal mines and farmland, which were both areas in which women worked as hard as, if not harder than, men. So she grew up seeing this reality, which, to her, seemed at odds with the way women were otherwise treated. Her mother was a 'pre-war human' and regretted not being able to get an education or job for herself, so she wanted Tsunoda to have those things. She urged Tsunoda to 'not stop work' if she had children, and to live as freely as possible under Japan's post-war constitution. Her mother was an avid reader, so Tsunoda grew up surrounded by books, and picked up her mother's habits of reading. Her mother died before Tsunoda's legal career began.

Tsunoda's contribution to Japan's feminist movement was always as an activist lawyer, even if her legal career arose, ironically, as a result of labour market sexism in 1960s Japan, as will shortly be explained. Tsunoda attended a public high school in Kokura in which a mere 30 out of 500 students per year level were female, with most having dropped out after junior high school. Nonetheless, Tsunoda remembers a male teacher complaining that there were too many female students in the school. Tsunoda went on to study Japanese literature after graduating high school, and then continued on to higher education to become qualified as a Japanese-language teacher, which resulted in her successfully obtaining a teaching license. But then she encountered difficulty: when she approached the Tokyo education bureau to ask about registration procedures to organise her employment as a teacher in the public school system, she was told they were no longer taking applications from women for Japanese-language teaching positions, because there were already too many women in these positions. They would take applications from female registered teachers only for science, technology, or maths teaching positions, and not for positions teaching English or Japanese language. Although Tsunoda had envisaged becoming a high-school teacher, this path was thus closed to her, and so she realised she needed to quickly re-train for another profession, and one in the humanities, given her educational background to that point. She realised that applying for standard, non-professional jobs in Japan as a woman was going to be near impossible. So, she came to the conclusion that law was her only option, and so went on to study for the bar exam, which can be taken by non-law-faculty graduates in Japan. In the beginning she could not attend law school classes even as an audit student because of the student protests at Tokyo University in the late 1960s (see Eckersall), so began her studies at home on her own steam. When classes finally recommenced, she had to scramble to study the curriculum quickly enough to sit the bar exam, which she did two years later. The classes she audited at Tokyo University's law school usually incorporated 50 students, of whom 2 or 3 would be female. Tsunoda officially registered as a lawyer at age 30, which made her one of the mere 3 per cent of female lawyers in Japan in the early 1970s. (Still today, this figure does not exceed 20 per cent.) Tsunoda had grown up never seeing a female lawyer, neither in real life nor in the television programs she watched as a child. When she first started out, police often mistook her for a wife of a detained criminal seeking a visit.

From 1986, Tsunoda worked as a consultant for the Tokyo Rape Crisis Center (*Gōkan Kyūen Sentā,* TRCC). The TRCC still operates today (see http://www.tokyo-rcc.org/), and Tsunoda continues to contribute to its work, but the Center is hardly known within Japan, even nearly 40 years after its founding. Throughout her career, Tsunoda continued working on behalf of sexual violence victims in civil cases, and in 1989, she launched Japan's first ever successful civil suit on behalf of a sexual harassment victim in the Fukuoka district court. After its favourable 1992 verdict, she lobbied the government to implement sexual harassment law, but to no avail. As is clear from her discussion below, sexual harassment is the form of sex discrimination that continues to be at the front of Tsunoda's mind and activist efforts. Her most recent book publication, with feminist lawyer Itō Kazuko, was specifically on the topic of sexual harassment in Japan.

Tokyo Rape Crisis Center

If an 'activist' is someone who speaks out publicly, then I suppose I would be called an activist, and this activism, which I've mostly done as a lawyer, has focused on sexual violence and sex crimes as an overlooked problem in Japan. I've done this legal work not just in the courts, but also in terms of speaking in public, and publishing written work about these issues. I've done this work mainly out of necessity, which led to me becoming an 'activist'. But, given that I was born and raised in Japanese society, I was not necessarily concerned about sexual violence from a young age. Rather, in the late 1960s, I took law classes at Tokyo University—as an audit student—in preparation for the national bar exam. At that time, law was a completely masculine field: it adopted nothing but the male viewpoint throughout its curriculum and all of its other facets. In criminal law classes, rape was covered, but, both in the lectures and their accompanying curriculum materials, it was described wholly from a male point of view. I was a diligent student, so I duly took on this perspective that completely dominated the descriptions and analysis that we were given. I took it on because I had nothing to consult in life outside of the university to compare the textbooks with, or to draw from to judge whether or not they were correct. So, I just believed what the professors said, and, unthinkingly, took on their teachings as fact. So, in the late 1960s, my understanding and consciousness in regard to rape was more or less the same one as Japanese men held at that time.

But, in 1986, I began volunteering as a legal advisor to the Tokyo Rape Crisis Center, and this was the first time I came into contact with women who spoke about their own experiences of rape. Through listening to these women, I came to realise that the understanding of rape I had gained from criminal law classes at university was entirely different from its ground-level reality. It was obviously the case that the accounts of survivors more accurately captured its true experience, so I gradually came to realise law school had taught me lies about rape.

The TRCC was set up by a handful of women in Tokyo in 1983 as a small operation. These founding women had been to America and learnt of women's organisations there that had been set up for rape victims. They saw that similar services were needed in Japan, and so started the organisation with just a few staff. They knew that direct, ground-level consultation with victims of rape was needed to organise services and support for them. They had no start-up capital, and launched the organisation using money sourced from meagre donations.

Three years later, in 1986, they had run out of money, and had no more donations coming in, and so decided to wind up the organisation. I'm not sure of the details, but, somehow, an *Asahi* newspaper journalist learned of their plight, and wrote an article about the organisation deciding to disband. The article appeared in the 'ladies household' section of the newspaper—as was always the case back in the 1980s—rather than in any social affairs section, which tells you a lot about the time: that such a significant social problem was relegated to a trivial women's issue. I had a home subscription to the *Asahi* newspaper back then (but not anymore!), and so read the article and was surprised to learn of the organisation and its planned closing. I had no idea that such things were happening in Japan at the time.

The article said that the TRCC was appealing for donations to keep the organisation running and to stave off closure, and, while I had no idea about the field, I nonetheless had some inkling that losing such an organisation would be a bad thing, and so I sent them a roughly 30,000 yen donation. Then, a staff member contacted me to meet up, which we did, and she asked me to consider acting as their legal advisor. The TRCC did, though, put one condition on this offer: that I wouldn't act as legal counsel for any accused rapists during my time with their organisation.

Of course, at the time, there were hardly any female lawyers in Japan; it would have been unusual for a female lawyer to be asked to act on behalf of an accused rapist anyway—male lawyers took care of that kind of case. So, fulfilling the TRCC's requirement in that respect was no trouble for me at all, and didn't impact on anyone else either. So I became a TRCC 'legal advisor' (*hōritsu komon*), which was a title grander in name than reality!

The TRCC at that time ran a victim telephone hotline, and, among the women who rang, there were some who requested an introduction to a lawyer and the like. The TRCC would refer such women to me. So, via the TRCC, I ended up having the chance to speak directly with victims, and this led to me launching civil cases on their behalf to secure compensation from perpetrators. The TRCC retained a few female lawyers like me for this work, and each of us, via the TRCC, ended up having substantial opportunity to liaise with victims as a result. From speaking with victims, we came to learn of the hostility of Japan's judiciary towards women, and how little support victims received in general. Japan's judiciary was antagonistic towards them. I'm still involved in the work today, and, through this work, I've come into contact with other feminist campaigns and organisations.

Learning From American Feminists

Through my work with the TRCC, and coming to work in the legal field of sexual assault, I came to realise there was nothing written in Japanese on the topic. When I first began initiating civil cases on behalf of victims for compensation, the biggest hurdle we faced was producing for judges expert research comment on the kinds of harms that victims of sexual assault suffered. Judges at the time had no idea of these harms of sexual violence, and so looked to me to provide them with research on the topic. Of course, I would explain to judges these harms, but my testimony didn't have the weight of research-based scholarship. I looked for this literature, but found almost nothing in Japanese. But the TRCC women found sources from America, in the field of psychology I think. There already existed in America an area of psychology that examined post-traumatic stress disorder (PTSD), as a result of victims having come back from the Vietnam War. TRCC staff members searched the journals to find articles for us lawyers, which we translated and used in court cases in Japan. This is how we managed to bring evidence-based opinion on the harms of sexual violence for victims, rather than relying on their emotional testimony. This scholarship ended up being very helpful in court.

I managed to find one book in Japanese published in 1979 that had been translated from French. A Tunisian female lawyer in France had compiled a record of court cases in which she had represented rape victims. The book's title in French means 'choice' (see Nakayama). Through this book, I was able to learn of statements about harms to sexual assault victims that had been made by lawyers in French courts, and these statements often drew on scholarship, and evidence from doctors and the like. We used this information in our own court cases, and it was very helpful.

CATHARINE MACKINNON

In the course of leading court cases on behalf of victims who came to me through the TRCC, I had come to know of Catharine MacKinnon, and the fact that she had been first in the world to theorise sexual harassment. I didn't know of her work until long after it had been published, but I came to realise that she was a world leader in terms of undertaking court cases relating to sexual harassment, assisting victims, and writing scholarship in this field. But she was not known in Japan, and the field in Japan had not yet developed at all, and so I realised I had no choice but to go to America to study with her directly. So I travelled to the US in 1994, and, during the time I was away, the topic of sexual harassment began to appear in small articles in legal journals in Japan. This process had begun with the earlier US supreme court decision on sexual harassment in 1986, which MacKinnon had been responsible for.[1]

The Fukuoka district court sexual harassment case, which ran from 1989 to 1992, was the first of its kind in Japan. I wanted to leave for America only after the trial was complete, and so, in 1992, when the case was won, I realised I could finally get away, and so I left in 1994. At the time, I didn't know anything about Catharine MacKinnon except her name, and I didn't know where she was based in America, and so I asked a number of local Japanese legal academics who had been to international conferences and the like, and one of them told me she was at the University of Michigan. Japanese custom is that we would normally

---

[1] The US supreme court case *Meritor Savings Bank v. Vinson* (1986).

have some kind of letter of introduction written by a mutual acquaintance when approaching someone like MacKinnon, and so I asked around as to whether anyone knew her personally, but there was no one. Then a colleague told me letters of introduction weren't so crucial in American culture, and that writing a letter directly from myself would suffice. So, I gingerly composed a letter, and got a reply! In the autumn before I left, I'd heard that MacKinnon was scheduled to give a series of intensive classes at the University of Michigan, and so I planned my trip around attending those. A secretary in her department told me which hotel I should book near the campus in Ann Arbor. Once I arrived, I approached MacKinnon with my plan to hopefully spend a year at the university as a research scholar, and I told her of the work I had been doing back in Japan. MacKinnon immediately got on the phone to the university study abroad administrator, and I met with them the following morning. The research fellowship was arranged, and I found myself well looked after by the university, because I was an unusual type of visiting scholar, due to my experience having already acted in court cases on behalf of victims back in Japan. So, they got me to speak to students about what was happening in Japan and give presentations on topics in Japanese law.

There were actually quite a few other exchange students from Japan in the department when I was there, from Japan's judiciary and the police, but when we were called upon in a class about legal aid to talk about the situation in Japan, no one volunteered, and since I'd had some contact with the system in Japan, I stepped forward. So I had to ring some of my contacts back in Japan to ask whether there existed any materials in English explaining Japan's approach to legal aid, and they sent me information that I was able to use in the tutorial. I got praise from everyone for the work I had been doing back in Japan, and this was the first time I'd ever been praised for it—that had never happened in Japan! I was able to refer to the TRCC as a 'rape crisis' organisation, and everyone instantly understood what I meant, which also wasn't the case back in Japan. I had always had to explain the nature of the activities of the Center, and everyone treated my legal work on its behalf like it was a marginal hobby on the edges of the profession.

Before I left for the US, I had a series of private English-language lessons to prepare for, and when the teacher asked me what kind of materials I wanted to practice with, I said that I wanted to cover topics like sexual harassment, sexual violence and rape. But nothing existed in Japanese on these topics, so the English-language school sourced

American-filmed television programs to use as teaching materials, like '60 Minutes' and similar current affairs shows, and the first one they showed me was a report of the 1986 sexual harassment judgement being delivered in court. There was nothing theoretical in Japanese on these kinds of topics, and no researchers working on them at the time, even fewer than today. But I was able to see from the television programs that the topic had already gained significant attention in America.

Japan Lagging Behind the World

Even now there is no clear definition of sexual harassment in Japanese law, which is a big problem. Japan has ratified the Convention on the Elimination of All Forms of Discrimination against Women (CEDAW), and even though Article 1 of the Convention defines 'discrimination against women', Japanese law does not, even now. Therefore, every time there is a country report on Japan produced by the CEDAW committee, it calls upon the Japanese government to establish a definition in law of sex discrimination. There exists a definition of rape in Japan's criminal code, but it is extremely narrowly defined, and so survivors want to overturn it, and replace it with a definition that better reflects the crime of rape as it is actually experienced by victims. This was a big topic of discussion in the recent Ministry of Justice committee that assessed the Penal Code amendments (see Chapter 3).

Women's sex-based rights and protections are not taken up as topics of legal discussion in Japan. University law faculties are mostly made up of men, and the criminal law academic association is filled with men. These men are extremely resistant to reform of Japan's rape law. There are historical reasons for this, and Japan's criminal law, since its development after the Meiji restoration in 1868, was entirely a project of men. Women didn't begin entering Japanese universities until after the war, and so the legal profession was carried on by men from the viewpoint of men, and in men's interests, for over fifty years. Women's sexual victimisation was conceived of in this context, which established a solid and entrenched basis for its definition, and this understanding of violence against women has since been very difficult to shift. But those who take up criminal law as a scholarly field in Japan have no idea of this history, and don't learn about it. They think that they're pursuing an academic field that is correct and right, without understanding its history, and so they don't question the legitimacy of Japanese criminal law against standards of human rights established internationally. So, from the point of view of women's human rights, and in terms of sex crimes, Japan finds itself not up to standards operating abroad.

In 1991, my book *Sei to Hōritsugaku* (*Sex and Jurisprudence*) was published with Yūhikaku Press, and it attracted some attention from women readers, so had 10 print runs. The Press's female editor, Michida Mitsuko, was the one who asked me to write a book on the topic. At first I hesitated, but it was my area of interest, and there was no one else who would write on that topic in Japan, and especially not from the point of view of women's sexual agency. Yūhikaku Press is a traditional legal publisher in Japan, and most of its editors are male. They told Michida that they didn't believe any such book would sell, and apparently she had a hard time getting the go-ahead for its commission. But she stuck with it, and the book was ultimately published. And it was successful to the point of being sold out. These days I'm approached by law school graduates in activist circles who tell me they read the book during their years at university. It's held in university libraries. I wrote about things that weren't being taught in Japanese law schools, and so the book ended up being useful for its unique perspective. But this doesn't mean it was used for teaching purposes in law schools. This was because academics didn't realise they were missing the perspective of the book in their curricula, and, besides, they had no interest in that perspective anyway. Academics who do have some interest in the topic probably do recommend the book to students as a secondary reading, but it isn't formally on any law school reading list in Japan. From the perspective of the orthodox legal academic field, the book is essentially incomprehensible.

Most sexual harassment incidents in Japan are dealt with via civil court action supported by Article 709 of the Civil Code.[2] This is the only recourse available to victims in Japan. I think this is a big problem, because Japan doesn't have any civic rights provisions like America's Title VII, and so victims who want to pursue sexual harassment claims in the courts have no option but to launch tort action under Article 709. But, as Catharine MacKinnon says, this kind of solution is a problem because it reduces the issue to the individual, when, in reality, even though the crime

---

[2] This article facilitates tort claims, in respect of the fact that '[a] person who intentionally or negligently violates the rights of others shall be liable for the loss caused by the act'.

of sexual harassment is perpetrated and experienced at the level of individuals, it's not actually a crime between individuals, because it's a problem of sexual exploitation, and so court cases involving adversarial action among individuals are not suited to the nature of the crime. But, because there has been no other option, I've spent my whole career pursuing such court cases, and I just wrote a journal article on the topic, but I've realised the extent to which this path of action has serious limitations. I think Japan's legal fraternity bears some responsibility for this situation. Pursuing the path defined in Article 709 has limitations, and it leaves victims collectively unaided. But lawyers, and even the female lawyers representing victims in civil action, aren't aware of this reality—they have no idea. They think they've been successful once judges order damages be paid, and when they've worked out how much money victims must receive. They see their role wholly as one of providing evidence of sexual harassment so that this compensation can be secured, and they see their job as finished once this money has been delivered. On the basis of Article 709, sexual harassment becomes a problem encountered by the individual, and the problem is contained within, and restricted to, the courts who deliver judgements to individuals. Its reality as a social problem of sex discrimination therefore never comes to light, and its cause—sex inequality in society—isn't ever recognised. Even with hundreds of civil cases found in favour of victims, nobody turns their mind to the problem as one of sex discrimination. This is despite the fact that sexual harassment is occurring daily in Japan, but even if all these cases reach the courts, their fundamental, underlying cause is left unaddressed, and lawyers continue their court actions over and over. When I was first starting out, I didn't realise any of this, and so I pursued the same path of civil action on the basis of Article 709. But as time progressed, I started to question the situation, and, even though I was achieving wins for victims in court and securing them compensation payments of tens of thousands of dollars (as paltry as that was), victims actually achieved very little through those court cases. They were left physically and mentally incapacitated in many instances, and the court cases didn't fix this. In most cases they launched court action only after leaving the jobs where they were harassed, and after effectively having to 'retire' from the labour market altogether. Then they were subjected to two- or three-year court cases that were emotionally draining, and only after that did they 'win'. But when, after 'winning', I looked back on what I had secured for those women, I felt that they'd achieved very little in the way of help and assistance.

I brought my thoughts on this situation to academic forums like the Japan Association of Gender and Law, but received little response, and I've written about the problem in various venues, but my analysis attracts no attention. Everyone just chalks up the court wins, even while establishing no legal definition of sexual harassment in Japanese law. It doesn't matter how many court wins we have, the law doesn't change, and no progress is made. No questions of the sex-unequal society that produces the problem in the first place evolve, as long as sexual harassment is a phenomenon of the civil courts and individual cases. Problems of discrimination in Japan, like racism and discrimination against leprosy victims, are all taken care of by Article 709, and no consciousness of their human rights dimension emerges as a result. Different from America, which has instruments like Title VII and Title IX, we have no similar structural mechanism for bringing these problems out of the courts and into the social realm of human rights. At most, victims can get financial compensation for mental distress, and, if they're lucky, a year's worth of lost wages. There's never any progress to discussion of what might be needed, socially, to deal with the problem of sexual harassment, such as that which exists in countries abroad where tribunals and other mechanisms are established. I certainly feel conflicted in accepting civil cases, but I do so only because there's no other option for victims at present in Japan.

Lawyers in Japan think all problems of discrimination should be dealt with as matters of Article 709. Even when I introduce MacKinnon's thinking that these problems of sexual harassment shouldn't be dealt with using individualised mechanisms like civil suits, the reaction I get— whether I talk at academic conferences or publish in scholarly journals—is always the same: silence. Lawyers seem happy just to be making money out of the cases.

Dignity as Relevant to Crimes of Sexual Violence

In terms of bringing a different viewpoint to this issue in Japan, we have the concept of injured 'dignity' in the constitution, which refers to harm inflicted on a person as a result of injury or lack of personal protection, whether on body or mind. Bodies like the United Nations and the Swedish government are comprehending sexual violence in this kind of way, but there's no similar understanding of it in Japan. There are international standards of human rights, but, as Shimaoka Mana has discussed,[3] these are not reflected in Japanese law. Just before problems arose within the Science Council of Japan (when Council nominees were vetoed by government),[4] on 30 September 2020, when members of the Council were discussing sexual violence cases in Japan's courts,[5] I submitted the opinion to the Council that Japan's relegation of sex crimes to Article 709 contravened international human rights standards. The Council agreed with my submitted opinion on this. However, even though the Council holds this view, legal academics in Japan don't accept it. The current situation with regards to legal approaches to sex crimes reflects the fact that Japan is behind the world in every area of human rights, as reflected in its 121st ranking in the Global Gender Gap index. No matter the international comparator you look at, Japan is behind the rest of the world, whether it's vaccination rates or anything else!

But there are young people in Japan today who are beginning to see the problem in the way I describe it, even if they are extremely rare. I taught for 9 years in the Meiji University law school, and I held endless discussions with students on the things we've chatted about today, but the ideas don't seem to have taken hold among them. The ideas are just too foreign to Japanese law students. But there are at least a few people who, after taking my lectures over and over, do seem to have taken the ideas into their later careers, and, in fact, one of them works together with me now. Even having just one other person taking up the ideas in Japan is a blessing I think. Other students who took my lectures recently stepped forward to help our legal campaign against the university medical school female admissions discrimination case (see Toyama). One of these students is a legal consultant for the organisation Human Rights Now in Tokyo.

---

[3] A law professor at Osaka University.

[4] In October 2020, then-Prime Minister Yoshihide Suga did not confirm 6 of 105 nominees who were recommended to him for appointment to the Science Council of Japan. The unconfirmed nominees had disciplinary backgrounds in the humanities, and speculation arose that political discrimination was involved in decision-making. They remain unconfirmed at the time of writing.

[5] The Science Council of Japan delivered a report in September 2020 that recommended enactment of a consent standard for sex crimes in Japan's Penal code. See Science Council of Japan.

Action on Sexual Harassment

I'm keen to see law reform in Japan in relation to sexual harassment. The recent International Labour Organization convention 190 prohibits workplace harassment.[6] For Japan to ratify this convention, it needs to establish regulations against sexual harassment. Japan does not yet have any such regulations, and their enactment will be difficult with the current situation in law. But from the point of view of sexual harassment reform in Japan, the convention is very useful, and will mean Japan will have to draft a law outlawing sexual harassment. So, at this stage, we need to begin campaigning for this ratification requirement. But I find that activists aren't interested in such issues in Japan, or in campaigning for such a law. We should see the convention as international best-practice standard on sexual harassment. If Japan were to ratify it, we would have a lot more latitude to campaign against sexual harassment. But that aside, the minimum requirement for ratification is the enactment of a law outlawing sexual harassment, and so we will need, at the very least, a legal definition of sexual harassment in Japan. Even though we've got this opportunity, there are very few activists mobilising to push for this change in Japan, and the focus of the feminist movement is on reform of the Penal Code sexual assault provisions. We just don't have a big enough feminist movement in Japan that women are willing to split their energies between different campaigns. But, of course, the issues are connected, so, personally, I think we should pursue them in coordination. But there's no civil society sector that campaigns for a law outlawing sexual harassment. Even the convention has attracted no public comment in Japan. Japan abstained from the vote over the provision in the International Labour Organization, but the country does not attract international censure for such actions.

Female Journalism in Japan

In 2019, 'Flower demo' events began in Japan after a series of 4 court cases found sex offenders not guilty, and it was mostly female journalists—and mostly young women—who reported on these cases, which meant the information reached women who then mobilised in protest. Male

---

[6] See International Labour Organization, 'C190—Violence and Harassment Convention, 2019 (No. 190),' https://www.ilo.org/dyn/normlex/en/f?p=NORMLEXPUB:12100:0::NO::P12100_ILO_CODE:C190 (Entry into force 25 June 2021).

journalists didn't report such cases, because they didn't see their significance. There are increasing numbers of young women entering journalism in Japan, and their numbers mean that reports of sexual violence are less now being seen as someone else's problem, and are more likely to be reported. I think this background was crucial to the emergence of the 'Flower demo' movement. Up until just recently, there had been few female journalists in Japan, and these women, just like female lawyers, were in a position of echoing the views of the men who dominated their professions to survive in their careers. But, with the increase in female journalists at Japanese newspapers, these papers became more open to printing articles about topics relevant to women from the perspective of women. Back in 2019, after the series of court case judgements had come to light, we held a symposium to Tokyo to hear the views of female journalists on the situation, and dozens of them attended. I was quite surprised. This seemed a big change to me. These female journalists have since been committed to reporting on developments in the criminal law reform committee too.

Japanese newspapers 30 years ago didn't print the word 'rape' (*gōkan* in Japanese), and instead used the phrase 'crimes of violence against ladies' (*fujo bōkō zai*). It's only been in these last twenty years that the word rape has been used in media reporting. I've heard male journalists defend their decision to not use the word on the basis it would hurt the feelings of victims. But the extent of the harm that readers imagine victims sustaining is totally different according to whether the word 'rape' or *fujo bōkō* is used! They use vague words to cover up the nature of things going on. This applies also to the issue of the 'comfort women' covered in Japanese newspapers. When South Korean Kim Hak-sun first stepped forward as a survivor of military sexual slavery [by the Japanese military in World War II] in 1990, I had a small column in a *Kyōdō Tsūshin* regional newspaper. So, when her press conference happened, I wrote about it using the phrase 'raped by the state'. But when my column was printed, they'd changed it to '*fujo bōkō* by the state'! I complained about the change. I don't like the Japanese tendency to make everything vague and unclear.

There was always the problem of sexual harassment in Japan, but it was only once the phrase and the concept it named came into the country that women realised they could talk about their experiences in that way. This was the same with domestic violence. They came to realise they didn't have to see their experiences as shameful, but, rather, as violations of their human rights. Having the words to use is really important.

Even the phrase 'sexual harassment' has come into Japanese from English, and is used as a foreign term that allows its meaning to be vague and euphemistic, and this leads us to the situation where no definition in law is seen as needed. This has made me realise how much Japanese has allowed for sexual violence against women to go unaddressed, because the words for talking about it weren't available to women. If women can hear other women describing their own experiences of 'domestic violence' or 'sexual harassment', they can give a name to harms they themselves have experienced. And this is crucial for establishing the foundational cause of the problem, and for being able to mobilise women to do something about it. But Japan is a society that doesn't yet tolerate such things.

 I do, nonetheless, think things have improved in Japan since the founding of the TRCC in 1983. We've had the Penal Code sex offences amendments and the emergence of the 'Flower demo'. These kinds of social actions are spreading in Japan. After all, it used to be not heard of that a woman would speak in front of people about her experience of sexual violation. This would have been seen as shameful, but women do so now at the 'Flower demo' events. And, so, thinking about that, I do feel things have changed hugely in Japan. But we're still right in the middle of an ongoing process that started only 2 years ago.

CHAPTER 6

Mitsui Mariko: A Feminist Leading Feminists

Abstract This chapter focuses on electoral politics in Japan, and feminist activism in service of greater female political representation. Perhaps the most prominent advocate of women's electoral progress in post-war Japan is Mitsui Mariko, and her testimony contributes to the bulk of the chapter's discussion. Mitsui's early activities as a feminist are first described, including an important period of time spent in America. Her subsequent entry into party politics, notably as a member of the Tokyo Metropolitan Assembly, is discussed, along with the myriad problems this caused her professionally and personally. Her later creation of the Alliance of Feminist Representatives, which initially campaigned for electoral gender quotas, is discussed in reference to the evolution in Mitsui's approach to feminist campaigning. Her long-running court action against her former employer, Toyonaka City, which Mitsui eventually won, is also discussed as an indirect product of the feminist backlash that occurred in Japan in the 2000s, after the earlier passing of the *Basic Law for a Gender Equal Society*. Like Tsunoda in the previous chapter, Mitsui concludes her discussion with reflections upon progress made in Japan towards women's liberation.

Keywords Mitsui Mariko · Tokyo Metropolitan Assembly · Norway · Alliance of Feminist Representatives · International Women's Year

Action Group · Sexual exploitation · Arai Shoko · Toyonaka City · Right-wing anti-feminist backlash beginning in the late 1990s

Over the course of her life, Mitsui Mariko has participated in, and organised, an extraordinary range of feminist activities in Japan. Her activism in areas including the sexual exploitation of women and girls, and in increasing the number of women in politics, makes her well known and widely respected by feminists across the country. At age 73, she barely shows signs of slowing down.

Mitsui began her activism in 1976 by joining *Kōdō Suru Kai* (International Women's Year Action Group), a national feminist organisation that formed after the 1975 United Nations World Conference on Women, which sparked the UN Decade for Women. She was in her twenties then, and working as a high-school teacher after having graduated from the women's university, Ochanomizu University, with a degree in literature. Mitsui's initial forays into feminist activism focused on the issue of the sexual objectification of women—which is something she has continued to work to eradicate her whole activist career—including recently on the issue of prostitution. It was at a regular monthly Tokyo street protest and seminar on this issue where the second author met Mitsui. The group organising these events, called *Kaishun Shakai wo Kangaeru Kai* (Alliance for ending prostitution), formed in 2020 in the wake of popular entertainer Okamura Takashi's public remarks that sex entertainment customers should eagerly await the entry of young women into hostess venues after they had been newly made poor in the pandemic. This group, as well as *Femigiren* (Alliance of Feminist Representatives), a group which Mitsui founded, and which will be discussed at length below, has since supported Arai Shōko, a former Kusatsu town councillor who accused the mayor of sexual assault and was subsequently voted out of her elected position. As Mitsui mentions below, Arai was the first and only woman on the Kusatsu town council in 2019 when she was expelled.

Mitsui's opposition to male violence is informed by her time spent in the US in the 1980s. She spent 1982 on a Fulbright scholarship undertaking a master's degree at Colombia University in New York, where she met feminists campaigning for anti-pornography laws. She read Catharine MacKinnon's work on sexual harassment and prostitution and was impressed by the gains the movement in the US was making.

She stayed in touch with women she met at the time and continued exchanging ideas with them via fax and postal mail upon her return to Japan. On her return to Tokyo, her head was 'full of ideas'—ideas she took into her new role as city councillor after being elected to the Tokyo Metropolitan Assembly in 1987.

One of Mitsui's motivations for running for office was to change the culture of Japan's male-dominated society (Mitsui, *Sekuhara 110 Ban* 3). Her first speech at the Tokyo assembly pulled no punches as she drew attention to the chamber's huge gender disparity:

> Please imagine the following, everyone [...] that 118 of the 127 people sitting in the assembly were women and only nine were men. You would certainly think it was strange if all the members of the highest deliberative bodies with decision-making power in the government of Tokyo were women. (cited in Kaya 385–86)

Indeed, it was in large part thanks to her that, in 1988, the Tokyo Metropolitan Assembly became the first administration in Japan to add 'sexual harassment' to the list of concerns that workers could raise in complaint to the city's labour bureau. Before then, what now would be called sexual harassment was listed as 'other' (Mitsui, *Sekuhara 110 Ban* 73–74), and so workers were not prompted to speak up about this workplace problem specifically. Sexual harassment then quickly became the category attracting the second highest number of consultations, second only to complaints relating to 'part-time work'. In an unfortunate irony, Mitsui quit the Tokyo Metropolitan Assembly in 1993 after suffering sexual harassment by a fellow male member of the Japan Socialist Party.

By the time Mitsui entered politics, not only was she well versed in issues of sexual exploitation from her time in America, but she had also developed a keen interest in gender inequality in politics and electoral systems. In 1986, she came to be inspired by a country which had 40% of its national legislative assembly occupied by women at the time: Norway. And so began her study of Norwegian politics, and her dogged attempts to apply the lessons learnt in that country to her own country's gender unequal situation. Of the 14 books that Mitsui has published, 4 are about the Norwegian political system and women's participation in it.

Six months after her first trip to Norway in 1986, Mitsui founded the *Zenkoku Feminisuto Giin Renmei* (Alliance of Feminist Representatives, referred to by members as *Femigiren*), with the specific purpose of getting gender quotas adopted in Japanese electoral politics. Around this time, Japanese politics saw a surge of women elected to the Diet upper house and onto municipal councils. So conspicuous was this increase in elected women—which peaked in 1990—that the media called it the 'Madonna boom'. Doi Takako became the first female leader of a political party in Japan in 1986 when she rose to the position of Japan Socialist Party head, which was the political party that Mitsui would later join and represent in the Tokyo Metropolitan Assembly.

Despite these advances of women into politics, at the end of the 1980s they occupied only 17.5% of seats in the national parliament's upper house (which was in fact a huge increase from the 5–6% around which it had stagnated since the 1950s), and approximately 3% in the lower house. The situation in municipal councils was similarly dire. For councils or political parties to implement quotas at this stage, as *Femigiren* insisted, was ambitious, and reflective of Mitsui's all-in approach to activism, as her discussion below shows.

In later years, Mitsui began to see that pushing for quotas was an unrealistic goal in a country where the situation was so gender unequal that, even today, 20% of municipal councils have no women on them at all. As Mitsui's vision changed, so too did *Femigiren* begin to expand and deepen its activities. *Femigiren* is one of the few women's organisations in Japan whose group name features the word 'feminist'. It is made up of a group of approximately 200 women politicians from around the country, mainly from municipal councils, and mainly from the left end of the political spectrum, that support other women's organisations, and has a primary vision of increasing the number of women elected to office. The first author first met Mitsui at a *Femigiren* meeting in Tokyo in 2007.

In 2000, Mitsui was hired to be the director of the organisation *Steppu*, which is Toyonaka City's gender equality promotion centre. *Steppu* was established at a time when local municipalities across Japan were implementing gender equality ordinances in line with the newly enacted *Basic Law for a Gender Equal Society*. *Steppu* was part of Toyonaka's drive to create a 'gender-equal society'. The 1999 Basic Law, however, concurrently spurred a gender equality 'backlash' in Japan—which is understood as having taken the form of an organised attack on gender equality that was spearheaded by right-wing groups, such as the Japan Conference

(Mitsui and Asakura; Kano 51),[1] as well as conservative media (Kano 52) whose proponents claimed the climate of the time was 'extreme'. These reactionary groups sought to protect what they argued was the 'traditional family' and the gendered division of labour. Mitsui (Mitsui and Asakura 54) calls the Japan Conference the 'control tower' of the backlash.

This backlash meant that Mitsui's tenure at *Steppu* frequently involved arguments with council members who had vested interests in pacifying right-wing groups. Several of these groups masqueraded as concerned citizens and lodged complaints to the Toyonaka council about Mitsui and *Steppu*. Council members associated with these right-wing groups convinced the council to postpone, time and time again, the creation of a gender equality ordinance. In 2003, it was dropped from the council's agenda completely.

Mitsui's role at *Steppu* therefore ended in acrimony when, after Toyonaka City and the foundation that funded the centre capitulated to the well-orchestrated and targeted anti-gender equality attack from right-wingers, she was unfairly dismissed in 2004. She took Toyonaka City to court, and, after a 7-year battle, sued it successfully for unfair dismissal on the basis that, although the dismissal itself was not illegal because she was on a non-regular contract (*hiseiki*), the manner of the dismissal had violated her dignity (*jinkakuken no shingai*). She received 1.5 million yen in damages.

In 2021, Mitsui was awarded the Royal Norwegian Order of Merit in recognition of her work researching the Norwegian political system and how it influences women's political participation. This was, Mitsui later said, one of the very few times that her work had been positively acknowledged, and, after a lifetime of criticism and backlash, she was touched (Otsuka). We interviewed Mitsui Mariko on 25 April 2021 in Tokyo.

---

[1] The Japan Conference (*Nihon Kaigi*) is a nationalistic organisation formed in 1997 with its main purpose to see the Constitution revised, but also to ensure patriotism be instilled in education. Many members of the Japanese Diet, especially those with conservative political leanings, are members of the Japan Conference.

Feminist Beginnings and International Influences

My activist origins are in the 1975 International Women's Year. This was what inspired me to join *Kōdō wo Okosu Onna Tachi no Kai* (International Women's Year Action Group). I read about the organisation in the newspaper in 1975 and thought, 'That sounds great', so I went to meet them and join up.[2] There were lots of people there who had been in the media, like Higuchi Keiko, Ichikawa Fusae, Yoshitake Teruko, and the lawyer Nakajima Michiko. I was still in my 20s, and they sort of indulged me. We organised together, but I was working at the time as a teacher, so I was most focused on wanting to abolish gender inequality in education.

I believed that education was the most critical tool in addressing gender inequality. I wanted to change a number of things in the education system, including abolishing gender stereotypes in textbooks, getting rid of unofficial traditional school rituals that had been made up by male teachers and changing the roll call system where girls' names were called only after all of the boys' names. So, I was active in attempting to bring equality into education. As for the media, well, it's a form of social education, isn't it? So we staged protests against inequality in the media too. After that, I studied briefly in America, and returned to Japan, but faced a bit of a setback in my activism because of health problems, and because I had been away from Japan for a while.

I returned to Japan around the time the *Equal Employment Opportunity Law* was being drafted, and the labour study group within the *Kōdō Suru Kai* created the 'Group for making our own equal employment opportunity law'.[3] The creation of this group was in response to

---

[2] *Kokusai Fujin Nen wo Kikkake Toshite Kōdō wo Okosu Onna Tachi no Kai* was the group's full name when it formed in 1975. It changed its name in 1986 to *Kōdō Suru Onna Tachi no Kai* (Women's Action Group) and was often abbreviated to *Kōdō Suru Kai* (Mackie 176).

[3] The official group title was *Watashitachi no Koyō Byōdō Hō wo Tsukuru Onna Tachi no Kai* (Women's Group to Create Our Own Equal Opportunity Act, often abbreviated to *Tsukuru Kai*) (Mackie 177).

the government's bill, which we opposed.[4] We instead pushed for an employment equality law more like that found in Europe.

I got home from the US very bloated and sick. I had been really focused on gender equality labour issues over there, really intently. But then, actually, I came close to dying. I was sick for over 6 months. The dreadful *Equal Employment Opportunity Law* was implemented in Japan, which was a setback, but I did recover. But I had been away from the movement for a while, and, when I returned, the Japan Socialist Party—it was called the JSP back then, and was led by Doi Takako, and its deputy was a woman called Kaneko Mitsu—asked me to run for them. I was asked to run, and I suppose I had made a name for myself by then by being a nuisance at Japan Teachers Union meetings (*Nikkyōso*).

Then I happened to get elected, and so I joined the Tokyo Metropolitan Assembly. I wanted to do so many things related to my activism: gender equality in education, gender equality in the media, gender equality in labour—it was like playing 'whack-a-mole'. Everywhere I looked there was discrimination. But as I mentioned, I had been seriously ill. I had been in hospital for a long time. Thanks to being a municipal high-school teacher, I'd been able to take sick leave and return to my job, which is something most people in Japan can't do. And so, in the end, I realised that all I would do in addressing each individual issue in a 'whack-a-mole' fashion would be kill myself or ruin my health. But by getting to the root of the problem—in other words, the system—we can move forward. The movement to increase the number of female members in the Diet was born through this process. But before this, I worked as a teacher, and this also fuelled my activism.

Feminist Activist Teacher

When I was a high-school teacher, we were made to pour tea. I didn't do it, though. I remember an incident when a new person was recruited. After the written test, there would be an interview. I was on the interview

---

[4] When Japan became a signatory to CEDAW in 1980 it was obliged to create a law guaranteeing sex equality in the workplace and the EEOL was the result. It was a compromise between labour and women's rights groups, and the government and business. Feminist groups were critical of the law because they viewed it as favouring the interests of business and being deaf to the needs of working women (and most working men). See Kobayashi for a detailed discussion of this.

panel for recruiting staff and teachers. There was one other person—a man—on the interview panel. This man asked the candidate, 'At this school there are people who refuse to serve tea and people who do it without making a fuss. Which kind are you?' This happened at the second-stage interview for an English-language teaching position. It was said in my presence, right in front of me, for my benefit, surely! Every day I thought I would be fired. And in the staff room, every day, whenever anyone served tea, I didn't get any. And then this interview incident happened, so the whole tea serving thing was a huge issue for me. So, later, when I saw women serving tea in my work at the Tokyo Metropolitan Assembly, it made me so angry. Anyway, the interview candidate responded, 'I'm the latter'. That is, a person who will serve tea and not make a fuss. Of course she would say this! Becoming a teacher was a big deal for women. The candidate had probably put her life on the line to get that far and pass the test.

When I was a teacher, I began to see that teaching gender equality at school was an important type of education, but *social* education—like spreading ideas of gender equality in society—was perhaps even more important. What this meant for me was getting involved in fights against the sexual exploitation of women even while I was a teacher. In the 1980s, pornography in Japan was really bad. There were advertisements on trains hanging right in front of our faces with explicit pictures of women. We would protest this sort of thing. You know the 'sealed sections' of newspapers and magazines? They made us so mad. I think it might have been the *Asahi Shimbun*—I can't quite remember—but when you opened the newspaper's sealed section, it was filled with naked women, completely naked. We protested really hard against those things. The anti-porn movement in America, which was happening at the same time, and which I had learnt from when I studied at Columbia University, didn't have it easy. But I think our movement jumped at the chance to do activism similar to what was going on over there.

At the time there were 3 of us leading the movement against sexual exploitation: me, Nakajima Satomi—one of the women who started *Femigiren*—and Sakamoto Nanae. We were all teachers, and back then, teachers had a fair amount of spare time. Specifically, we campaigned against the sex tours to Asia, and mostly against the South Korean *kisaeng* tours, which were terrible. We re-named Jalpak *'yarupak'*,[5] because that's exactly what they were; the company even said so in its advertising pamphlets. The wording was vague, but the Jalpak tour pamphlets included promotion of that sort of thing [sex tourism], and it made us see red: the fact they were making these leaflets and handing them out. We were high-school teachers, so we taught sex equality, but this sort of thing—sexual exploitation—well, we thought our public activism was an even more effective form of social education than textbooks. I started removing sexually exploitative advertisements from trains and taking them to the companies' headquarters as a protest against women's bodies being treated like objects. I was warned I'd better stop because it was a crime to remove advertisements from the trains. I guess I could have been jailed for that crime but thanks to those protest actions, I was able to write about and publicise our activism. So, we truly put our bodies on the line in our activism in those days.

Feminist Activist Assembly Member

The three of us eventually formed a media group called 'Porn-watching', but, if I remember correctly, I was an assembly member at the time, and there's a limit to what you can do as an elected representative in Japan in terms of activism. Once I became an assembly member, my attention was drawn more to what was going on within the Tokyo Metropolitan Assembly in terms of its co-hosting of events like courtesan shows and the Miss Tokyo contest. The Tokyo governor would give a speech and crown the winner of the Miss Tokyo contest final, for example. So, I turned my scalpel to things like this that commodified women and exploited their sexuality.

The courtesan shows are dreadful, and continue today. There is a Tokyo tourist bus operator that goes to tourist spots, including Yoshiwara, where the old pleasure quarters were located. This operator had a tour that included viewing a courtesan show. These buses fell under direct control of the Tokyo administration because they were Tokyo buses, and I think they were funded by Tokyo. When I asked the bus company to stop doing courtesan show tours, I came under vicious attack for attempting

---

[5] Jalpak is the name of a package tour operated by one of Japan's leading tour companies, JAL. *'Yarupak'* is a play on words: *'yaru'* is a colloquial word to mean 'do', also used as a euphemism for sexual intercourse.

to obstruct its business. In the end, we had to compromise and accept the courtesan part of the tours, but we got the bus operator to include historical information that the courtesans in Yoshiwara were there as a result of severe poverty.

As for the Miss Tokyo contest, this was something over which I was attacked relentlessly. An organisation external to the Tokyo Metropolitan Assembly but attached to the Tokyo administration—so, basically, Tokyo—hosted these events like they were a natural occurrence. It wasn't unusual for local governments to run these things back in the 1980s. As to why I was attacked so badly, well, I secretly entered the Miss Tokyo contest as a contestant. Why did I do this? I had been asking questions in the council about many things, like the contest's budget, and saying that people's taxes shouldn't be used for such events. As a result of this questioning, they suggested changing a few things as a compromise. For example, they said that, instead of focusing solely on women's hip, waist, and bust sizes, or faces, they would choose a citizen of Tokyo who was a good representative of the city to use in campaigns and advertisements. Well, my friends and I thought, 'If it's just a representative, then age shouldn't matter, and even someone in a wheelchair should be suitable too!' We decided that a few of us should enter, so we each filled out an application form. But, when it got to the final stage of application, everyone but me had decided against it. They were worried about their jobs and other commitments in case something went wrong. So, I was the only one left. But we kept it secret, like underground activism. I was determined to keep the campaign under wraps and get into the pageant. I didn't tell anyone about my plans, but somehow a newspaper found out. I was so surprised. I don't remember the title of the report, but it suggested that I'd entered the pageant because I thought I had a beautiful face. This shocked me because I was hoping to send exactly the opposite message. The newspapers were bad, and the tabloids were worse. My friends knew the real story, but the mass media created the misunderstanding that I had entered the pageant because I had tickets on myself. I got a lot of horrible phone calls threatening rape and things like that. The incident made me aware of how difficult it is to protest something like that.

Femigiren: The Belief that More Women in Politics is Good for Women

As for my motivation for founding *Femigiren*, it was right about the time I became a member of the Tokyo Metropolitan Assembly. Back then, in the assembly, the female workers would serve tea that male assembly members would drink. I just got so angry, being exposed to this every day. (I brought my own mug.) Also, there were so few women assembly members and hardly any discussion about women's issues. So, I thought we needed more women councillors, otherwise things like women serving tea and sexual harassment would just continue. I was in my 30s and had experienced so much sexual harassment. I thought the 'whack-a-mole approach' of tackling each individual incident wouldn't solve anything and believed there needed to be more women in the assembly. That's why I set up *Femigiren*.

My motivations have changed a lot since then. I was—I don't know—naïve; I had no fear. I thought I could make things change quickly. I was following the United Nations activities and the activism in northern Europe, and I thought we definitely needed to get women to 30%. Critical mass is 30%, so I believed we needed to implement a 30% quota for all assemblies. I was very active in trying to get a target—I lodged complaints to different political parties, met with different people, and wrote submissions. This was in the 1990s, and back then there were a lot of assemblies with no women in them. And here I was trying to implement a target of 30% or 40%. Of course, aiming for a target is a good thing, but it was very unrealistic when there were so many councils with no women, or only one woman representative. Currently, a group of us run the 'eradicate councils with no women' movement. I was told that the term 'eradicate' was scary, so we used the cuter phrase 'get rid of councils with no women'. But we're trying to make sure there no longer exist councils in Japan with no female representatives, or merely one representative—like Kusatsu town council used to have. So, in terms of activism, I've shifted my energies towards trying to increase the number of women on councils.

It was only when we went into rural areas that we saw councils with only one woman on them, or none at all. Local women's groups need to adopt a localised style of activism. For example, there is the Tokushima group that aims to increase the number of women politicians, and then there is Takei Takako[6] from Ehime who is working very hard. We work very closely with local women who strive to get more women into politics; I share my experiences with them. In this way, connecting with the outside world is easier. Putting people in touch with each other is also something. So, there's a fair amount of detailed work, and lots of consultation. For instance, the campaign in support of the Kusatsu councillor, Arai Shōko: At first it didn't really look like expanding into a movement, but after some time *Femigiren* joined in the protest. But even before getting to that point, I spent a lot of time on one-on-one consultations with her, and providing information and support. I think these are also forms of activism.

One of *Femigiren*'s major successes was the introduction of a law aiming for gender quotas.[7] It took 30 years, but we were the first to include the introduction of quotas in our activist goals. At the time, people were like, 'What? Quarter?' and couldn't even pronounce it—the word itself wasn't yet known by anyone. Now, even though it's not like we have a functioning quota system like the Scandinavian countries, people can at least say the word 'quota' correctly, and the concept has become normalised in the media and in political parties. This is because we, right at the beginning, briefed political party leaders on the matter, submitted letters, and spoke up everywhere about quotas. This sort of activism gave rise to the current favourable climate in Japan towards quotas. International movements were also very influential, probably more so than *Femigiren*. But *Femigiren* started the conversation about quotas in Japan during a time when no one knew about them. I guess you could call this a success, maybe. But we don't actually have quotas in Japan yet, after all! But at least the term has taken hold and people are talking about it; I think this is a success.

---

[6] Takei Takako served as a member of the Matsuyama City council for fifteen years before becoming a member of the Ehime Prefectural council in 2017. She is a long-serving member of *Femigiren* and is very active as an explicitly feminist politician in promoting women's issues and raising awareness about sexually discriminatory practices in councils.

[7] *The Act on Promotion of Gender Equality in the Political Field (Seiji Bunya ni Okeru Danjo Kyōdō Sankaku no Suishin ni Kansuru Hōritsu)* was implemented in 2018. It is referred to unofficially by some as the *kōhosha danjo kintō hō* (candidate gender equality law), and this is the term Mitsui used.

The most prominent group that *Femigiren* is associated with is *Q no Kai*.[8] The activism leading up to the enactment of the 2018 candidate gender equality law was led by, initially, Akamatsu Ryōko,[9] as the group's representative, as well as academics, Diet members and others. And *Femigiren* also had its own members involved.

Diet members who are in *Femigiren* are usually quite active, down-to-earth people. Politicians and former politicians—I'm also a former politician—are quicker to action than thoughts, and I think this is important. This capacity to mobilise came into play in the lead-up to the candidate gender equality law.

Taking on a Local Government and Winning

Perhaps one of my most significant battles was the one I had with Toyonaka City. Despite the significance of this court case, I am rarely asked to talk about it. Perhaps this is because the incident is complicated. Even when the court case was taking place, it was complicated. I called the media and briefed them in the hope they would understand what was going on, but I was told several times that the issue was too hard to cover. It was actually an extremely unusual case because we won in the supreme court against Toyonaka City—a local government! That itself was unusual, but the nature of the case made it even more so. My dismissal and the City's failure to rehire me weren't judged by the courts as illegal. But the reason I was fired was due to extreme, organised, and continual pressure applied by an assembly member, the kind who associates with the Japan Conference, and the courts recognised this. It was only 1999, and the Japan Conference had just formed, so not many people paid attention to the kind of organisation it was or the kind of

---

[8] The group's full name is *Kuōta wo Suishin Suru Kai* (Group that promotes quota systems).

[9] Akamatsu Ryōko was one of the first women to work in the Japanese bureaucracy in the Ministry of Labour, and eventually came to hold the position of head of the Women's Bureau inside the Ministry of Labour, before eventually becoming the Minister of Education. She was one of Japan's delegates to the United Nations for three years from 1979 and was instrumental in the implementation of the *Equal Employment Opportunity Law* in 1986. In an effort to see more women elected to political office, in 1999, she founded the organisation WINWIN (Women in the New World International Network), which is based on the U.S. Emily's List, and today, at the age of 92, she continues her activist work in promoting greater female political representation.

activities it was engaged in. Local governments were drafting ordinances to promote women's issues, and it was these gender equality efforts of local governments that the backlashers came after. And I think this was hard for people in the media to understand because of the lack of understanding of the nature and even existence of the backlash. The trial went on for 7 years, and I became completely exhausted. My support group included over 800 people, so it was a very large movement. Also, because it was Toyonaka, a local government in Osaka, it didn't get as much attention in other parts of Japan as perhaps something similar might have had in Tokyo. The incident was covered very widely in the Osaka area, but didn't really make national news, and this might also be a reason why people don't know about the case or ask me about it.

Progress and Reflection

These days I'm involved in various activities, including a group that rallies for ratification of the Optional Protocol to the Convention on the Elimination of All forms of Discrimination Against Women. Also, *Femigiren* sends a representative to various causes, and so I liaise with those people and bring back information from them. Also, as needed, I go on marches with these groups outside the Diet; I also usually attend their meetings too.

Compared to 30 years ago, there is less ridicule of feminists in Japan today, and we're taken more seriously. But there's still a long way to go. In particular, I think television still generates the big 'water cooler' conversation topics in Japan, and so I think it's important for the television networks to cover elections in a more easy-to-understand way and make programs that cover women and politics more deeply and treat them more seriously.

As for the general public, I think there is increased awareness of gender inequality generally. For example, the issue of separate surnames: In Japan, married couples must legally have the same surname.[10] In response to this, in all the surveys, women—well, not only women, but particularly women—believe the law is not right. And many people believe that it would be better if there were more women Diet members. Well, it's only natural that women think like this; it's probably only Japan that has this

---

[10] See Chapter 3 for an explanation of this issue.

situation. So, yes, there have been changes. In a survey the other day, I think it was 90% of women in their teens and 20s who agreed that couples should have the option of having separate surnames. I thought, 'There you go!'.

But in general, the situation is terrible, really dreadful. But if I say that, then I, and the other activists, have to reflect on that. What could we have done to change this terrible situation? I suspect there was another way? I wonder if we weren't competent enough. At any rate, in my opinion, the situation is really terrible in many areas, but particularly in labour. More than half of all people working are non-regular workers, right? And now with the pandemic, they've really been left out in the cold. Many women work in the service industry, and now those working at the front line of healthcare—the care workers, like nurses whose jobs are low paid and hard work—are having to quit. I think these are the biggest problems, and I really wonder what to do. But I feel like I'm always getting angry, and this isn't good for my health.

As far as progress goes, it's not like I've conducted a survey or have objective data, so I can't really say anything substantial, but, looking around, I think there's been an increase in the number of women who are willing to go to court over things they think are wrong. And I feel like there's been an increase in the number of women willing to run for office—more women candidates, mainly in local politics. So, in this sense, I believe there have been steps in the right direction.

Women in *Kōdō Suru Kai* were thought of as women libbers. What I remember vividly is how women in the women's liberation movement were called 'ugly women with inferiority complexes' (*busu no higami*), and I remember this because I thought it was such a great phrase. We nonetheless thought of ourselves as women's libbers. These days we call ourselves feminists. I went to a reasonably intellectual university—Ochanomizu University. I remember my friends from there reacted as though I had said I had AIDS when I told them I was a women's libber—it was a real turn off. They would gossip about me. That's what it was like back then—the word 'lib' itself was really disparaged. In that respect, I think things have changed quite a bit. People don't really talk behind your back anymore as a feminist. But back then it was like you were a strange insect.

CHAPTER 7

Yang Ching-Ja: Seeds of Hope

Abstract The wartime 'comfort women' issue continues to animate large parts of Japan's contemporary feminist movement, with groups and individuals rallying in support of survivors, against the right-wing reactionaries who attack them, and in pursuit of apology, reparation, and public education. A prominent leader of these efforts in Japan is Yang Ching-Ja, and her testimony forms the basis of this chapter's discussion of contemporary thinking and campaigning approaches to the history of Japanese military sexual slavery. The chapter canvasses the evolution in Yang's approach to the 'comfort women' issue from the early 1990s, and philosophical outlook on what motivates acts of political solidarity with these victims. This evolution brought about Yang's eventual co-founding of the organisation Kibōtane, and the chapter describes the activities of this organisation in light of Yang's conflicting views of feminism and shifts occurring in women's identification with feminism in Japan. The December 2015 Agreement over the 'comfort women' issue concluded by the Japanese and South Korean governments had a big impact on Yang and the Japan-based advocacy movement, because it resulted in their alienation from Japan's broad left. In the chapter, Yang reflects on changes in her activism since 2015, and lessons learnt from her long-running involvement in survivor Song Shin-do's court cases against the Japanese government. The chapter concludes with Yang's thoughts about the influence of the South Korean 'comfort women' advocacy movement on contemporary Japanese feminism.

Keywords Yang Ching-Ja · Kibōtane · Comfort women · 'Zainichi' feminist campaigning · Korean Council · December 2015 Agreement · Song Shin-Do · Youth study tours to South Korea · 'Flower demo'

We interviewed Yang Ching-Ja at her office, shared with her husband, in Nishikokubunji in April 2021, just as she was moving to a different location and up to her ears in boxes. Even in such busy circumstances, Yang was her typically composed, friendly self, which is a disposition that serves her well in her many and varied pursuits. The second author came to know Yang through events held by the Violence Against Women in War Research Action Center (VAWW-RAC),[1] and through Yang's numerous research publications on topics relating to the Japanese military 'comfort women' sex slaves of World War Two. Yang was 63 years old at the time of the interview, and juggling university language teaching at Hitotsubashi University, interpreting, activism, writing, and directorship of the organisation *Kibō no Tane Kikin* or '*Kibōtane*' (Seeds of hope). It was Yang's leadership of *Kibōtane*, and longstanding prominence in the 'comfort women' justice movement, that drew us to her as a voice of contemporary Japanese feminism. As her discussion below reveals, however, Yang's relationship with feminism is a conflicted one.

Yang is among Japan's longest and most thoroughly involved activists in justice campaigning for the former 'comfort women', and has an international profile that reflects this biography (see discussion of Yang also in Tai). She is a second-generation *zainichi* Korean-background-resident of Japan who came to campaigning, first, through co-founding the group Uri Yeoseong Network (Yeoseong Net), before the 'comfort women' issue came to global attention, and then through becoming a member of the group supporting Korean survivor Song Shin-Do's 10-year-long series of court actions against the Japanese government (see Seo). Yang in her earlier years features in a documentary film about these cases, titled in English *My Heart is Not Broken Yet*. She remains Japan's strongest link

---

[1] This organisation wound down its activities in 2021.

to 'comfort women'campaigners in South Korea as a result of her long-term friendship with the former director of the South Korean Council for Justice and Remembrance for the Issues of Military Sexual Slavery by Japan (the Korean Council), Yoon Mee-Hyang. Her ability to interpret simultaneously in Japanese and Korean also makes Yang central to events held jointly by activists in the two countries, and these events in the form of 'webinars' became more frequent in the pandemic. Long before, Yang interpreted for noted historian Yoshimi Yoshiaki in his 2007 research work interviewing 15 Korean 'comfort women' survivors (Yang, 'Katarenai Kioku Wo Kiku: "Ianfu" Sabaibaa No Katari' 123).

Yang's activism, writing, and public speaking is centrally and deeply focused on survivors and their perspectives, hardships, lives as activists, and relationship to the justice movement. Most recently she has described them as 'the first #MeToo activists' (Yang, 'Saguru/Fukumeru: Kim Hak-Sun San Kara Hajimatta #MeToo'), and suggested that survivor Kim Hak-Sun's August 1991 press conference was the true beginning of the world's 'MeToo' movement (Yang, 'Saguru/Fukumeru: Kim Hak-Sun San Kara Hajimatta #MeToo' 26). Her catalogue of writing is substantial, and takes the form of books, journal articles, and magazine pieces, especially published in Japan's left-wing press, over a 30-year writing career. Of all writing on the topic of the 'comfort women', it is perhaps Yang's work as a whole that ponders survivors most intensively, and in this respect her long-term activist collaboration with Kawata Fumiko is unsurprising.[2]

Yang's concentrated focus on survivors, and close connection to members of the Korean Council, meant her expertise became particularly useful to Japan's justice movement in 2020 when reactionary and misogynistic groups in South Korea successfully destabilised the local movement in that country through attacking Yoon Mee-Hyang after she became a ruling party lawmaker. In an August 2020 piece in Japan's widely read monthly magazine *Sekai*, Yang clarified misunderstandings that had arisen among Japanese activists about these dramatic developments occurring in South Korea (Yang, '"Seigiren" Basshingu No Kōzu: Hōdō to Jijitsu'). She alerted readers to the fact that survivor Lee Yongsu's critical comments at an earlier press conference about misused funds donated to

---

[2] Kawata Fumiko is well-known for her decades-long collaborations with 'comfort women' survivors, and for writing books that record their biographies in moving and sensitive detail. See, for example, her 1982 *Onna Tachi No Komoriuta*.

survivor representative organisations, which was a claim quickly assumed to be correct by South Korea's right-wing media and all media outlets in Japan, came only *after* right-wing attacks on Yoon Mee-Hyang had begun with her elevation to South Korea's congress. In other words, Lee's critical public comments, whatever their validity, merely contributed to, rather than sparked, an ongoing campaign against the Korean Council. Yang's defence of the Korean Council in her *Sekai* piece is, nonetheless, notable for its careful and sympathetic consideration of survivor Lee Yongsu's press conference comments, which she finds to be those of a victim in distress over a number of things, including Yoon Mee-Hyang's departure from the Korean Council.

The Korean Council has represented 'comfort women' survivors ever since Kim Hak-Sun stepped forward in 1991 and spoke on South Korean television about her sexual victimisation at the hands of Japanese troops during the war. The Council has been the major body in South Korea, and, indeed, the world, to advocate in support of apology, reparation, and public education on behalf of survivors like her, even at the United Nations. It has supported survivors, furthermore, to pursue civil action against the Japanese government, via courts both in Japan and the US. Yoon Mee-Hyang is the organisation's longest-serving and most prominent leader, and her passing of its directorship to Lee Na-Young (a professor at Chung-Ang University in Seoul, see Conclusion to this book) in 2020 spelt huge change for the Council, and a break with its extraordinarily successful history of the 1990s and 2000s.

Even more seriously disruptive of the justice movement in South Korea, however, as Yang emphasises in her discussion below, was the 28 December 2015 South Korea-Japan Agreement on the 'comfort women', which was a verbal arrangement between the South Korean and Japanese governments to refrain from discussing the 'comfort women' issue in international forums, and to discourage the creation of 'comfort women' public memorials, in exchange for a lump-sum amount transferred from Japan for the medical expenses of survivors. Yang describes the different direction her justice campaigning was forced to take after the signing of this agreement, which wedged justice campaigners even in Japanese progressive circles. While the Agreement is now defunct after the Moon Jae-In government took power in 2017 and dismantled it, it nonetheless dealt a blow to activists in both Japan and South Korea whose organisations, incorporating survivors, had been excluded from negotiations, and whose ability to appeal to international bodies was curtailed by the agreement. As Yang explains, the Japanese left (or 'liberals', as she calls them) turned on justice activists for opposing the agreement because their opposition was seen as obstructive of Japan-South Korea diplomatic reconciliation. Developments in 2015 in this way marginalised the justice movement, and, as Yang describes, this ostracisation continues to the present day.

Through *Kibōtane*, however, which is an organisation promising 'seeds of hope', Yang hopes to reverse this situation through recruiting a new generation of 'comfort women' advocates who understand the achievements of survivors as political activists, and properly comprehend the role of supporters of these survivors over the past 30 years. The hackneyed allegation that survivors are 'used' or 'led-on' by advocacy organisations and the activists who campaign alongside them is shown to be nonsensical, in Yang's view, once the decades-long political leadership of 'comfort women' survivors themselves is properly understood. The 'comfort women' justice movement is, after all, the biggest social movement to have emerged in Asia after the end of the war, and its most prominent organisers and public speakers are survivors themselves. Thanks also to decades of activism by supportive campaigners like Yang Ching-Ja working alongside these now-elderly women, Japan's contemporary feminist movement, with its upcoming generation of young women, has a great deal to build upon, and very many seeds of hope to reap.

The December 2015 Agreement

I was already involved in a number of activist organisations before launching *Kibō no Tane Kikin* (*Kibōtane*), with the most prominent one launched in February 2010, called *Nihon-Gun 'Ianfu' Mondai Kaiketsu Senkoku Kōdō* (Japan Nationwide Action for the Resolution of the Japanese Military 'Comfort Women'). This group amalgamated a range of groups and individuals working on the 'comfort women' problem in Japan, and continues now effectively as an umbrella alliance representative organisation. It works with the South Korean Council for Justice and Remembrance for the Issues of Military Sexual Slavery by Japan (the Korean Council) to seek resolution to the 'comfort women' problem. This involves, primarily, lobbying the Japanese government and attempting to influence legislation.

But, with the 28 December 2015 Agreement, in the form that it took, the Korean Council became really discouraged in this activity, and so did we. Roughly around that time, the Korean Council, on the encouragement of groups and individuals gathered around the organisation, merged with an already-existing group to form a new organisation, which is why it changed its name [from the former Korean Council for the Women Drafted for Military Sexual Slavery by Japan] to its current one. This merger occurred in 2018. This new organisation is focused not just on the previous aims of getting the Japanese government to recognise the crimes of the past, apologise to survivors, and compensate them (as are the standard aims of 'comfort women' advocacy groups in Korea), but, in addition to these goals, it now prioritises research into the historical facts of the wartime sexual slavery system, and education towards preventing its reoccurrence. These are the publicly proclaimed goals of the new organisation.

Because of this stance, our response to the 28 December 2015 Agreement was to say that it should represent just the beginning to a resolution of the problem. But the Japanese and South Korean governments declared the agreement the 'final resolution'. This, of course, is an approach that promises no resolution to the problem at all. It was insufficient even just in respect of recognising historical crimes and apologising to victims, let alone in respect of our other aims. Survivors aimed for no such crimes to ever happen again, but the agreement offered no guarantee of any such eventuality. In respect of the aims of the newly amalgamated organisation, including historical research into the facts of the war crimes and future prevention efforts and public education, the agreement contained no provisions that satisfied the organisation whatsoever.

So, at that point, we decided that we could no longer wait for the Japanese government to fulfil obligations that it had been called upon to meet over many years, especially given that survivors were dwindling in number. So, we decided that we would forget about the Japanese government and our demands of it, and instead work towards efforts towards resolution of the problem ourselves. We would do this on the steam of the citizens of each respective country. Enthusiasm to take this different path was palpable from the time the agreement was brokered.

I had been campaigning in Japan, and up until the signing of the agreement in 2015, had been lobbying the Japanese government and proposing various legislative models. But the agreement came at the end of all those efforts, despite our work over so many years. This caused us quite a bit of consternation, and destabilised us, especially with survivors advancing so much in age. We were in a state of panic about the campaign and what we should do. On reflection, we had been looking for a top-down solution to the problem.

The South Korean Constitutional Court in 2011 had ordered the state to take action on the 'comfort women' issue, and the South Korean government subsequently did so. This became a chance for local activists, and so a top-down approach was pursued in Korea. In Japan, on the other hand, we scrambled to find an approach to campaigning that would lead to resolution of the problem. In the end, we found that our aims did not have the support of the Japanese people. The country was under the rule of the Shinzo Abe regime, which was a government that bluntly refused to acknowledge historical facts. In an environment of pressure created by this kind of government, and the December 2015 Agreement that it produced, activists realised that our desire for a top-down solution was wrong, and it was time to revise our approach.

At this point, I thought it would be better to *directly* change the minds of the Japanese people. This would involve an approach of talking to people face-to-face. We had to take this new approach because we believed we no longer had the support of the Japanese media, and so the public was being given a message wholly different from ours on the topic of the 'comfort women'. With the December 2015 Agreement, we activists were labelled by this media as too 'idealistic' and unrealistic. Even local Japanese 'liberals' (*riberaru*) no longer supported our viewpoint (and I know the term 'liberal' has a specifically Japanese meaning in political science terms). So we were no longer able to get our viewpoint into mainstream media outlets. I took the view that we needed to reach out directly to young people in Japan. We needed to tell them directly about the harms the 'comfort women' victims suffered, and we needed to do this through victim testimonies about their experiences of wartime sexual violence. In other words, through the voices of victims themselves.

By this time, many survivors had already become publicly known activists who would speak out in the media. There are, of course, many survivors who never became activists, and this group is in the majority. In South Korea, there were 240 officially registered survivors, and just a tiny proportion of these women became activists. In the beginning they were at their limits just talking about their own experiences of harm, but, gradually, over time, they became emotionally capable of speaking out more widely. As a result, they travelled all over the world to sites of military conflict where similar crimes against women were understood to be taking place. They spoke among audiences involved with campaigning on behalf of women sexually exploited around American military bases in South Korea as well. As they participated in this campaigning, their public statements began to change, and they became genuine political activists. We wanted to tell Japanese young people about this process, and the fact that the activism of survivors was being distorted in the media [to differently suggest that survivors were being led-on or duped by activists].

The media and public discourse at this time suggested that obstruction from organisations representing survivors was causing the 'comfort women' problem to remain unresolved. This kind of understanding of the problem was even more popular among Japanese liberals than the country's right-wing. They had the perception that the 'comfort women' problem needed to be quickly resolved in order that friendly diplomatic relations could resume between Japan and South Korea. Representative organisations were therefore seen as an impediment and obstruction to resolving the problem. In fact, the Japanese right-wing was more likely to welcome our activism because they were comforted by the thought it prevented good relations between Japan and South Korea! It was actually Japanese liberals who were most put out by our activism! For that reason, our perspective was never conveyed in the Japanese liberal media around the time of the agreement. Of course, though, neither did we get any airtime in the right-wing press.

Directly Engaging Japanese Youth

We were faced with having to take a different approach, and so I thought we had no choice but to begin to reach out to people directly with our message. We would have to convey not just the experiences of victims, but also knowledge of the campaigning that we had undertaken together, hand-in-hand, with survivors over thirty years. We had to tell young people about this 30-year history of campaigning. We had no means to do this but to talk to them directly. It would be a long, hard road, and our approach was a naive one with little prospect of results in the near future. But it was the only option we had in terms of campaigning. We had been robbed of any other means to reach a large audience through the media or through public institutions.

So, when we founded *Kibōtane*, we joined in alliance with the Korean Council in order to convey historical facts of the wartime slavery problem to Japanese youth. There are many survivor support organisations in Asia, but Japanese youth tend to have the impression that the 'comfort women' issue is wholly bound up in the politics of the Japan-South Korea diplomatic relationship. Accordingly, we decided to take Japanese youth to Korea, and have them interact with local youth, so that, together, they would have a chance to think about the issue collaboratively. We wanted to create chances for this kind of process, and so we founded *Kibōtane* in 2017.

In 2018, we held our first tour to South Korea for Japanese youth. In 2019, we held another 2 tours in spring and autumn, but, in 2020, with the onset of the pandemic, we were unable to continue. So we ended up holding just 3 tours in total. But the tours produced huge results, I think, looking back. When we announced the first one, I wondered whether we'd actually get any applicants, but we worked hard to attract some. We had higher numbers of applicants the second and third times. We made sure the tour fee was very low—around 20,000 yen—for the 3-night and 4-day tour. We set the fee at 20,000 yen in the beginning, because we felt that making the tour completely free might attract applicants who were just looking for a holiday. But we ended up attracting groups of young people who had known about the 'comfort women' issue in broad terms, but had always wanted to learn more about it.

Unexpectedly, the youth who joined the tours were most happy about the fact that they got to interact not just with South Korean youth on the issue, but were also able to meet fellow Japanese youth, who were also interested in the issue. This was a surprising outcome. They had felt alone, and different, for being interested in the 'comfort women' issue in Japan, and so were happy to find, though participating in the tours, other young people of a similar mindset. This made us reflect on the extent of the isolated and frosty environment that exists in Japan surrounding the 'comfort women' issue. Attention to the issue had vanished almost completely.

We advertised the tours and recruited participants via the *Kibōtane* website. Alternatively, university professors directed students to our website and call for participants. There aren't many teachers talking about the 'comfort women' issue in Japanese high schools, but the topic is still talked about in a number of Japanese universities. We aimed for 15 participants for the first tour, but got 20 applicants, so we decided to take them all. Although, shortly before embarkation, the parents of some of these participants stopped them going, and some eventually couldn't go for other reasons, so we ended up with 16 on the first tour. We recruited for 20 participants for the second tour and got 23 applicants, so we took them all along. The third time we recruited for 20 participants and got 25, but, because we found 23 participants in the previous tour arduous, we had to turn down 5 applicants and take only 20. But, on this third tour, too, we had the parents of one applicant oppose their participation in the end, so we ended up taking 19. Most of them were women.

I teach Korean language at university, and I touch on the comfort women issue in my classes. I find that male students are more likely to take on the issue as one of geopolitics and diplomacy between Japan and South Korea. I don't know why, but male students have a tendency to see the issue as one of national interest. Female students, on the other hand, are more likely to take on the issue in a bodily way, through understanding its sexual violence, and they are able to imagine more directly its implications for young women like themselves, or for girls younger than themselves, in a physical way. I think this different way of interpreting the issue had an effect on the sex-breakdown of participants in the tours.

In 2019, we additionally got some external project funding to run a Japan-South Korea youth cooperation project. From the 60 or so participants in the tours over the two years, we chose 10 people to enter a second stage of activity. This would involve spending one year in dialogue and debate with Korean youth to come up with ways to spread awareness of the 'comfort women' issue among young people. The project would aim to create concrete outcomes. We had funding, so we recruited 10 participants each from Japan and South Korea, 20 in total. All 10 applicants from Japan were female. (We put out the call for participants among the 60 or so youth who had already participated in the tours.) This result, of course, was affected by the fact that, in the first place, it was women who were the majority of participants in the tours. On the Korean side, too, all participants were female. So this project run last year was wholly a female affair in the end.

I don't call myself a feminist, but, through campaigning with *Kibōtane*, I've begun to feel that Japan has changed in respect of the fact that, among the participants in the joint Japan-South Korea project we ran last year, there were Japanese female participants who openly called themselves feminists. Not all of them, but there were definitely some who were forthright in calling themselves feminists, and so this made me feel that, these days, there are more young people who feel like they've got a personal connection to feminism.

Feminism and 'Comfort Women' Campaigning

We've just started a new project that looks at the activists in Japan who have been campaigning on the 'comfort women' issue for many years. In this project activists are interviewed about their experiences of campaigning over the past 30 years. Japanese activism has been outwardly led by people like me and Kim Puja, but there are activists who have been involved in, and working consistently hard, for over 30 years in the background of the movement this whole time.

A unique feature of Japan-based campaigners in support of the 'comfort women' is their consciousness of belonging to the perpetrator country. So campaigners here support victims not only from South Korea, but also from other countries, like the Philippines, China, and Indonesia. Activists take it upon themselves to support victims in each of the respective countries. There have been activists doing this unrecognised, unrewarded work over decades, and the project we started this year involves young people interviewing these activists. Just last week they interviewed Kawata Fumiko.

I just mentioned the fact that many young women involved with *Kibōotane* call themselves feminists, and there are female participants in this year's project team, too, who call themselves feminists. Ironically, though, Kawata once authored an 'anti-feminist manifesto'. Feminism for Kawata wholly equates with Ueno Chizuko, who is too liberal and middle class for her. Kawata was raised poor, and, so, given Ueno's style of theorising, she feels like Ueno speaks from an elevated position, and isn't able to understand the experiences of people who are poor and how they feel. She doesn't reflect this ground-level reality in her theorising.

In the past, it would have been the case that calling oneself an 'anti-feminist' in front of a feminist would have led to an argument, but these days young people are not likely to respond in any such way. For them, being a feminist is a natural thing, and something you just arrive at as a result of living in the world as a woman. This is a generational difference, I think. When I was a high-school student, the women's liberation movement emerged in Japan, and I was a big fan of it. I had an image of women in this movement as wearing helmets and cool street-protest gear and confronting men. I really felt affinity with them. But in university I got a chance to read some feminist theoretical texts, and their content was difficult. I couldn't understand them. But I felt affinity for liberationists outside of these difficult texts who I imagined were confronting the same kinds of problems that I faced in my own life as a woman. And I wondered why the texts unnecessarily made things complicated. It was after this that my enthusiasm for feminism began to wane. Kawata is older than me, but I imagine that for women of her generation feminism emerged as an elite movement. Ueno was representative of this elitism, and she dominated feminism in Japan.

I'm a Korean-national Japanese resident, and, living in Japan, I feel excluded first on that basis, even before feeling excluded on the basis of being female. This is something I feel intuitively. With the recent incident in Japan involving discrimination in examinations for female applicants to university medicine departments (see Chapter 2), I had the response that it was a terrible situation, and I was glad feminists rose up in reaction to it, but, from my point of view, along with men, I've been similarly excluded in Japanese society on the basis of being Korean. I can't help this kind of thought coming to my mind when I hear of incidents like the medicine department case. This is one reason why I can't get fully on board with feminism.

Another reason relates to the fact that—and this might be a bit disrespectful towards feminists—I attended a Korean school in Japan, and am a 2nd-generation Korean resident of Japan. My parents came from Jeju Island. But I was born and bred in Japan. The school I attended was fully aligned with North Korea, even if Korean schools in Japan didn't start out with any such tendency. We were taught that the Democratic People's Republic of Korea was paradise, and learnt about Marxist Leninism from primary school. More specifically, we learnt the teachings of Kim Il Sung. Everything was about ideology. Ideology, ideology, ideology! In this context, there were teachers who had completely swallowed Kim Il Sung-ism and no longer thought for themselves, and ended up doing silly things. So, I think I was brought up with an acute understanding of ideology. It's unfair to put feminism in the same box, but I saw it as another 'ism'. I did read some feminist texts after entering university, but, when I found them hard to read, given this pre-existing suspicion I harboured of ideology, I found myself not able to get into the feminist ideas contained in them. There were lots of feminists in Japanese cities back then, and, when I had a chance to ask them about why they became feminists, they would always tell me that the world became clear to them through feminism. But the same kind of thing is said of Kim Il Sung-ism—that the world becomes clear through the lens of his ideas.

This made me see feminists as telling the same kinds of lies as my teachers did back in school.

There were feminists in a group that I was in that supported the court case of the former Korean comfort women Song Shin-Do, and one of them—a good friend of mine—was a journalist and connected to the feminist Japanese magazine *Femin*. I was talking to her one day, and happened to say I wasn't a feminist. I certainly wasn't an anti-feminist, but I felt I didn't know enough about feminism to call myself one. But when I said this to my friend, she told me I was a feminist and just didn't realise it. At that point, I thought she was probably right. Even if I didn't understand its finer points, and even if I couldn't relate to the kinds of things Ueno Chizuko said, and even if I didn't feel like the world became crystal clear through a feminist lens, the way I was living my life led someone to confirm to me that I was a feminist, and I was able to agree that I was. I was still exactly the same person that had been attracted to women's liberation in my earlier years, and I was dissatisfied with the hardship that women faced living in Japanese society. Even though I was mainly involved in the 'comfort women' problem narrowly, I did want to change society. It was hard to live in Japan as a Korean, but it was also hard as a woman. My friend was different from the feminists who would react in a hostile way if I said I wasn't a feminist, and would think that I was therefore an anti-feminist. But my friend just kindly replied with her different view that I actually was a feminist. I was really grateful for that reaction, because I couldn't have come to that conclusion myself. I was happy for her confirmation, but I wasn't able to say it for myself. I came from the generation that thought someone had to study a great deal before they could call themselves a feminist. But young women today call themselves feminists on the basis of their self-regard, and, when I interact with them, I feel like we've had different lives in that respect. I think there's lots of feminists of my generation who don't call themselves as such. But today, even in Japan, it's become easier for women to call themselves feminists. There's not such a heavy emphasis on the definition of 'feminist' these days. But my generation thought someone had to have an internal definition of feminism to be able to call themselves a feminist. And because I couldn't come up with one, I wasn't able to call myself such. But when I ask young women today why they are feminists, they can't answer, and seem to wonder why I'm even asking the question. Feminism and women's liberation are distinct in my mind.

Early Activism

I got married after university to a 2nd generation Korean Japan-resident man, and had two children. For the 2 or 3 years after they were born, the most I did was translation work from home. I wasn't active outside the home for these years after their birth. But I gradually got sick of being at home, and, just around this time, some *zainichi* girlfriends from my university days got in touch. *Zainichi* women tend to love catching up with each other, but, at that time, I didn't really have that kind of burning desire. It's awkward to admit, but I don't tend to be someone who keeps up with people, but I do have trouble turning down invitations to catch up. Plus, they proposed that the 5 of us catch up regularly to begin studying the 'history of the Korean people'. I thought that I wouldn't have much chance to do such a thing while stuck at home, and I had been wanting to escape the house a bit, even though I had absolutely no interest in the 'history of the Korean people'. But since they were kind enough to invite me, I decided to join.

Among these 5 women was one who had studied in South Korea—Yamashita Yeong-e.[3] She had studied the 'comfort women' issue under Yun Chungok's supervision, and was back in Japan for a short while. This was 1990. She told us Yun Chungok was scheduled to speak in Japan in December. This was to become, of course, a historic lecture. It led to a group of *zainichi* women subsequently coming together to pursue the issues raised in the lecture, which I was invited to join. Among its participants, me and Kim Puja were the younger ones. Kim Puja wasn't in the earlier 'history of the Korean people' study group, but she was part of this later group. By this stage, Kim Puja was more of an activist than me—she had been involved in lots of *zainichi* issues.[4] Four of her associates additionally joined the group, which aimed to take action after Yun Chungok's lecture, rather than just abandoning the lecture as a one-off event. The 'comfort women' issue ended up being proposed among

---

[3] Professor Yamashita Yeong-ae is a well-known scholar of the 'comfort women' based at Bunkyo University, and has published a body of literature on the topic, particularly in collaboration with South Korean colleagues, most prominently Yun Chungok.

[4] Kim Puja is a professor at Tokyo University of Foreign Studies, and, as a professional historian, is a central figure in Japan's contemporary feminist movement, as an activist, writer, researcher, and public speaker. She collaborates closely with Professor Onozawa Akane at Rikkyo University, who, as a professional historian, is equally central to contemporary feminist organising on topics like the 'comfort women' and prostitution.

the topics addressed in Yun Chungok's lecture for continued action in this group because it was a problem of history, which some of us had been studying.

The women who joined the group initially all came with different views, but there were many there who thought that, as feminists, the 'comfort women' issue was the one they wanted to bring to light as a problem of women's human rights. This topic became our focus as we debated various options for the group. My view at the time was that the big problem was one of historical consciousness. Of course, the 'comfort women' issue *was* a problem of historical consciousness, but it was also a problem of women.

When I was at home with the children, I made lots of friends with mothers living in the same apartment block. Once I became close to these women, they would invariably ask me why my family members and I all retained our Korean names while many of their other *zainichi* friends adopted Japanese names. They didn't know about our family background, and I felt that my children would end up having tough lives in Japanese society coming from the kind of family that we were, given the low level of awareness among the Japanese people of our history. Japanese people had created the historical circumstances that led to our family coming to live in Japan as residents, but they knew nothing about it. I had been feeling like I wanted to tackle this problem of awareness when I incidentally became exposed to the 'comfort women' issue. I felt like it was a problem tied to the history of *zainichi* coming to be the demographic it is in Japan, and that both the situation of the *zainichi* and that of the 'comfort women' were linked to the historical period of Japanese imperialism. I thought the 'comfort women' issue was a useful topic to use to convey to the Japanese people the harms that had been caused by the Japanese colonisation of Korea.

I'd never been an activist, and tended to be cynical about everything, and was under the impression that activism couldn't be undertaken on behalf of others: one had to bring one's own aims to it. Otherwise it wouldn't be sincere. Accordingly, in relation to the 'comfort women' problem, I saw it as a vehicle to convey to Japanese society how difficult it was to live as a *zainichi*, as well as a woman. In fact, living as a woman meant that I faced hardship both within the *zainichi* community and within *zainichi* groups, as well as in Japanese society. And I felt strongly at the time that the 'comfort women' issue was a good way to convey this dual problem.

At this time, Kim Hak-Sun, the first woman to speak publicly of her experiences as a 'comfort woman', had not yet come forward in South Korea. So when we had the meeting to decide on the focus of our group, we all debated and spoke at a million miles an hour, which was typical of us *zainichi* women! The 5 of us debated what we would do for months without coming to a conclusion.

Kim Puja and I were in our 30s, and were the youngest members of the group, which was mostly women in their 50s. There was a big gap between *zainichi* women in their 30s and those in their 50s in those days. The ones in their 30s had all graduated from university—at least the ones involved in the group had. In other words, they had been raised in families that were keen to send even daughters on to higher education. But the ones in their 50s had never been to university, and they had been forced to work so that their bothers could attend instead. Even when they'd been smarter than their younger brothers, they had to work, and they were conscious of this fact, deep in their bones. As a result, they railed against any injustice they saw, and had to verbally call out anything and everything bad about the world. They were distorted by feelings of blazing anger. Or at least this is how we saw the women 20 years older than ourselves. But we, 20 years younger, and having graduated university, were more magnanimous in our outlooks. Our schooling wasn't too distorted by the old ideas of education being useless for females. However, once we left school, then we suddenly encountered sexism— the kind of sexism that treats women differently on the basis we're female. So there was a divide between the two groups—between those who had experienced sexism from birth, and those who encountered it later.

Those of us in our 30s discussed the 'comfort women' problem in theoretical terms, as one of a problem of women and human rights. We decided to focus our campaigning on it in order to force Japanese society to discuss the issue. So we planned for public debate over the issue from the outset. As I mentioned, I hadn't been an activist before that point, but Kim Puja had, and so had Kim Yeong-Hee.[5] They had campaigning experience, and so were impatient to get things done, and not mess around. We agreed to disband the group once the 'comfort women' issue had been taken up as a topic of discussion by the Japanese public. We went backwards and forwards over what name we should give

---

[5] Kim Yeong-Hee subsequently created the organisation *Ridoresu Kokusai Kyanpēn* (Redress International Campaign).

ourselves: debating whether *'Chōsen'* or *'Kankoku'* [as different names for Korea] would be better, and during our messing around over this naming issue, Kim Hak-Sun stepped forward as the first Korean survivor in 1991. Then the issue became a Japan nationwide debate. So we were no longer in a position to be messing around worrying about our group name, and we worked to make sure we weren't left behind in the public discussion that was unfolding. And so we went with the name Uri Yeoseong Network ['We women'] to avoid making any choice between *'Kankoku'* or *'Chōsen'* before our November 1991 launch.

At the time, there was Kim Hak-Sun's emergence [as the first 'comfort woman' to speak publicly] and then her court case, and this became a focus of public discussion, but in Japan everyone was more concerned about how much trouble the issue would cause for Japan, and how much information would come out about the crimes of the past. We were obviously worried about this tendency in the public debate, and wanted to inform Japanese society just how big a human rights violation this history was for women. As such, we first decided to publish a book, although our first actual activity as a group was a signature petition in support of Kim Hak-Sun. In preparation for the book, I made my first ever trip to South Korea to talk to survivors. I'd never been there before, and my nationality had previously been North Korean. But, just before that time, unrelatedly, I had switched my nationality from North to South Korea—my husband did it first and I followed. Our children would then automatically become South Korean citizens. Having them remain as North Korean citizens made us feel too uneasy. It was around this time when I was asked to go to South Korea to gather testimony from victims that I finally decided to organise my South Korean passport. I was aged 34, and that was the first time I'd ever had a passport.

Lessons from Survivors

So I went to South Korea. From that trip, I learnt a lesson from survivors that was to remain indelibly emblazoned on my brain: my pre-held idea that the 'comfort women' problem was an issue of colonialism was wrong, and I wouldn't be able to use this issue to campaign in my own interests as a *zainichi*. That was the only model of activism I had comprehended at the time, and I thought that not doing it that way would wrongfully result in my doing humanitarian charity work, rather than political work. But I realised how wrong my thinking had been once I actually met with survivors. I realised their lives had been indelibly changed by the experience of having been made into 'comfort women'. They were extremely impoverished as well as living in significant mental distress. I was able to see these things clearly only after meeting them.

It absolutely wasn't a matter of these women having experienced hardship as a result of having the same generational background as other Koreans in terms of being female and having lived through the Japanese colonial era. Their situation was wholly and starkly different from even those who had survived this level of historical disadvantage and hardship. I realised I couldn't leave their experience undistinguished from that of broader issues of colonialism that I felt were more relevant to my own situation. So I realised I had to raise my voice on behalf of myself and my own issues, but, in relation to their situation, it wasn't the case that I should tie it to my issues, or make myself part of their cause, but, rather, I first should work to assist them and their struggle to overcome their experience and circumstances. I realised this was what was needed.

Subsequent to that, as I continued campaigning, my biggest quandary came in relation to the Japanese activists in the movement who felt responsibility for the 'comfort women' history on the basis of being Japanese, and members of the perpetrator nation, and so participated in campaigning on the basis of this motivation. But I wasn't Japanese, and I'd had everything I thought I'd known theoretically about activism overturned upon meeting survivors. I'd been proceeding from the outset on the basis of my own personal theory of activism. So I really found myself at point zero. But, in order to be able to continue with activism, I had to figure out for myself why I was doing it; I found myself questioning my own motivations. In the beginning I was able to easily give a theoretical answer whenever anyone asked me why I was involved in campaigning, but, once I returned from South Korea, I found myself lost for words whenever I was asked. I'm not someone who thinks about things too deeply, but, one day, even without thinking about it too much, the answer came to me like a bolt out of the blue: I had a responsibility to be involved in campaigning because I'd gained knowledge of the situation of the 'comfort women', and because of this fact, there was no escaping my obligation to continue with campaigning on their behalf. They were victims in overwhelming terms—becoming involved in Song Shin-Do's court action support team made me realise this.[6]

SONG SHIN-DO

There were so many times I wanted to run away from involvement in Song Shin-Do's court action support team—interactions with her were very difficult. There was so much that people like us—who had lived lives of normality—didn't understand, and so we didn't understand her reactions to anything. There was no possibility that we could relate to her through extrapolating any of our own experiences, and trying to do so was a waste of time. We couldn't bring to our activism that kind of thinking. No matter what we did and how many times we did it, she would criticise and hassle us, and people around us didn't understand this, and so they would give us endless advice about how we should improve our ways. But, of course we couldn't respond to people by explaining the reality of the situation, so we found ourselves stuck in a constant dilemma. We really had a tough time. I wished many times to leave the group, but I always caught myself, and realised that I didn't want to become the kind of person who had knowledge of what the 'comfort women' had been through but would abandon their responsibility to do something about it. I wasn't able to leave because I had knowledge of a group of people who had been terribly abused, and this imposed on me an obligation to continue.

When I came to terms with this fact, things were instantly easier for me. I came to realise, simply, that the reason I campaigned was, plainly, because I was not permitted to stop. Because I wanted to fulfil the responsibility that I bore. From that point on I was campaigning not for any higher purpose, or for myself, but simply because there was no other option. At this point, I was much more at ease as a campaigner, and simply understood within myself that I would continue as long as I had an obligation to do so. And this is still the case for me today. I still have a

---

[6] Song Shin-Do, who died in 2017, was the most prominent Japan-based survivor of wartime military sexual slavery. She was born in Korea, but remained in Japan after the war. In the 1990s, over a ten-year period, she pursued civil claims against the Japanese government, all of which ended in defeat. Song was also active in speaking to Japanese children in schools about wartime history. She is the subject of the 2009 documentary film *My Heart Is Not Broken Yet*.

sense of wanting to discharge the obligation I have towards the 'comfort women'.

KIBŌTANE IN THE CONTEMPORARY JAPANESE WOMEN'S MOVEMENT

Kibōtane is fully a 'comfort women'-focused organisation. There are many young people involved with both *Kibōtane* as well as *Femizemi*, which is obviously a feminist organisation in Japan. The organisers of *Femizemi* are involved in the 'comfort women' problem as younger-generation researchers. We at *Kibōtane* have some personal connections with members of *Femizemi*. *Kibōtane* has recently held online seminars free for students, and we get 100 people attending every time. For our upcoming testimony project [as mentioned above, interviewing long-term activists], too, we've got 30 participants, and news of our initiatives spreads widely among these young people.

Nagayama Satoko, who is involved with *Femizemi*, used to be involved with *Kibōtane's* management, and there are contacts of hers who are now involved across the 2 organisations. And vice-versa: some of our participants were involved with *Femizemi* first, but are now involved with *Kibōtane*. But, at its heart, *Kibōtane* is a 'comfort women' organisation, and so people involved in the 'comfort women' issue give us the most support. Also, *Kibōtane's* director Kitahara Minori is obviously a feminist activist, and it was she who asked me whether I wanted to be involved in the initiative from the outset. She's right at the heart of feminism in Japan, and very impressive.[7] It was me and Kitahara who organised the initial support campaign for Itō Shiori. But now, Kitahara is not so involved in that, and, in fact, just 2 days after we formed the support campaign, she created the 'Flower demo' campaign! And then she left the support campaign without consulting me! But it's Kitahara's role in *Kibōtane* that links the organisation to Japanese feminism. A further connection to the 'Flower demo' is *Kibōtane's* role as the local seller of Marymond 'comfort women' social enterprise fundraising products in Japan. Obviously Marymond's central focus is flowers, and so, apparently, this connection was in Kitahara's mind when she chose the protest movement's name.

---

[7] See Chapter 2 for Kitahara Minori and the 'Flower demo'.

'Flower Demo'

Before I founded *Kibōtane,* I was involved in the fundraising campaign for the creation of the Korean Council's War and Women's Human Rights Museum in Seoul, and this involved conducting tours for adults in Japan to South Korea. Kitahara participated in a number of these tours. The tours first involved a visit to the museum, and after that to one of the sex industry districts around the US bases in South Korea to listen to the stories of victims. Another destination was a facility for women who had survived sexual exploitation by local Korean men in prostitution. There we listened to the staff of the organisation who supported these survivors. The tour focused on listening to women involved in South Korea's feminist movement. I went a number of times. As a result, via these tours, we got to see a great deal of the South Korean women's movement, and this influenced the later creation of the 'Flower demo'. The tours gave us inspiration for how these things could be organised. We learnt that women could be mobilised via social media. We learnt these techniques from Korean women. Kitahara was a major bridge to bringing the insights of South Korean feminism to Japan.

The 'Flower demo' has been a major development in Japan. I intended to attend its first event, but it ended up being very cold that day, so I didn't go along! I had finished teaching one of my university classes, and it was going to take an hour to get to Tokyo station, and the weather was freezing cold. I really regret not going along. The survivors who tell their stories at the events are not under any compunction to do so; they do so because they want to. At first, the event format was to have an organised speaker list beforehand. But what happened was that, even after the planned hour had ended, people at the 'Flower demo' event stepped forward afterwards to take the microphone themselves because they wanted to tell their experiences of hardship in their own words. This happened the first time the event was held. It makes me even more regretful I didn't attend. As a result, though, 'Flower demo' events became opportunities for people to step forward spontaneously to speak about their experiences of sexual assault at the microphone. There are people who speak about such experiences from decades ago. This shows how sexual assault is never forgotten, not even decades later, by victims. This is the same as the 'comfort women' problem in that survivors are unable to forget sexual assault that happened decades and decades before, which of course is understandably the case. How does one forget sexual assault, even after 30 or 40 years? It's impossible. This parallel between the 'Flower demo' and the 'comfort women' movement is obvious to Kitahara too.

But the achievement of the 'Flower demo' movement in facilitating the public testimony of women really is something unimagined in Japan, totally unexpected. This kind of event emerged in South Korea, too, as part of the 2016 Gangnam Station murder 'post-it-note' movement in Gwanghwamun Square. The fact that 'Flower demo' participants were not forced in any way to tell their stories publicly, but nonetheless did so proactively, shows how desperately they wanted to, and how much they needed a place to do so. This latent demand came to the surface through the events, and for this reason they are a revolutionary development in Japan. In the case of the 'comfort women', the Korean Council already existed [by 1990], and so Kim Hak-Sun was able to come forward with her story [in 1991]. In the same way, Japanese victims have been able to come forward because of the advent of the 'Flower demo' movement. It's not that survivors had been hiding and silent, it's that victims who wanted to tell their experiences needed a place to do so, both in Japan and South Korea. Korea was the first to provide survivors with this place, even before Japan.

The South Korean Women's Movement

I think South Korea's women's movement is stronger than Japan's because patriarchal oppression is stronger in that country, even stronger than in Japan where it is surprisingly not felt by many people. Younger women in Japan today are more aware of the problems, but women of my generation, when we were their age, didn't have such awareness, and there were many who genuinely thought no sex discrimination existed in Japan. I knew them personally. For example, because I was busily involved in campaigning on the 'comfort women' issue, mothers at my child's school, when they saw my husband attend classroom parent observation days, would say to him, 'You poor thing, having a wife running free like she is'. This is what women would say! My husband would come home and joke about having been pitied by everyone. Of course, this would also have been happening in Korea at the time. I've never lived in South Korea, but the Japanese *zainichi* community was very Confucian and patriarchal, and so I can imagine it was similar in Korea. But in Korea, the sexism was more blatant, and identifiable; the oppression was more obvious than in

Japan. And I think this made women less able to bare it, and led to the earlier development of the women's movement there. Also, the history of South Korean political activism is different from Japan, and Korea had the democracy movement that fought for change on all fronts. Amidst the struggle for democracy, women's problems were put off for a later time, and, as is often said, the Korean women's movement was therefore led by the women who had participated in the democracy movement in the late 1980s. They brought forward problems of domestic violence and sexual assault to Korean society. But, before that time, during the democracy movement, the 'righteousness' of that movement meant that women's issues were put on the backburner, and left for another time. Democracy was made the first aim. To some extent this is understandable. But there were women who had cut their activist teeth on that democracy movement, and so as soon as it was achieved, they then raised the fact there'd been sexism and violence towards women in the movement. They were able to ride the wave of the democracy movement in this respect. In Japan, in contrast, women experienced no such history. I tend to think the post-war history of Japan (and not just the wartime/pre-war history) has a lot to do with how women in this country have ended up today.

I've promised to continue with *Kibōtane* till age 70, for the next 7 years, before I finish up. I don't know whether I really will be able to finish then or not. But, more seriously, I worry about how we can secure successors for our movement. Until now, I've been preoccupied with getting things done that needed to be done in the movement, but, recently, coming to terms with declining energy levels, I've become more focused on how to foster the next generation of 'comfort women' activists. And I've been feeling that we really need to properly make sure this is done, otherwise the work of the past 30 years will have all been in vain.

CHAPTER 8

Japan's Feminist Movement Within the Global Sisterhood

Abstract This concluding chapter reflects upon the decades-long decline in the status of Japanese women that has gone mostly unnoticed by the global feminist movement. It suggests that Japanese activists have attempted to strengthen their position through forging connections with South Korea's feminist movement, and the chapter notes a range of ways in which Japanese and South Korean feminists have collaborated. The chapter advises that feminists elsewhere should take the lead shown by Korean feminists in overseas efforts of solidarity, and it notes the many recent successes of the South Korean feminist movement. While South Korean 'comfort women' advocacy and anti-prostitution campaigning have been major areas of borrowing and collaboration by Japanese feminists, more recently the movement draws inspiration from Korean feminism across a span of ideas and topics, which the chapter touches upon in its second half. Even with support from South Korea, however, the chapter lastly returns to the task facing Japanese feminists in terms of exercising influence and reach in a country with a long history of institutionalised prostitution and pornography, and yet with limited feminist achievements in areas such as spy-cam filming. The chapter urges greater attention and support from feminists abroad in service of the efforts of Japanese feminists like those described in the book's 6 chapters.

© The Author(s), under exclusive license to Springer Nature Singapore Pte Ltd. 2022
E. Dalton and C. Norma, *Voices from the Contemporary Japanese Feminist Movement*, Palgrave Macmillan Studies on Human Rights in Asia, https://doi.org/10.1007/978-981-19-2228-2_8

Keywords Global sisterhood · Sexualisation of Japanese women · Success of the South Korean feminist movement · Ajuma Books · South Korean anti-prostitution activism · 4B movement · Anti-beauty movement · Tokyo Summer Olympics · Spy-cam filming · Japan's domestic pornography industry

Global sisterhood, as it is understood by feminist theorists like Maria Mies, refers to women's common cause all over the world, whatever their cultural, economic, or geographic differences. This common cause is, as other theorists like Carole Pateman and Catharine MacKinnon explain, liberation from the male rule that produces the sex class women. In Japan, this rule is by both local and foreign men. The foreign men are not just the tens of thousands of American troops stationed in the country, but also the men abroad who promote ideas of Japanese women as suited to prostitution and pornography; namely, as fetishised 'geisha' or sexualised comic characters (see Norma, 'The Geisha-Effect: Western Capitalisation on Japanese Commercial Sexual Exploitation'). This internationally coordinated campaign against Japanese women has a long history, and continues today in the form of worldwide trafficked pornography made of them or marketed in their guise. Sadly less coordinated has been any countercampaign by the global feminist movement to support the efforts of Japanese women to resist such impositions.[1] Inadequate feminist resistance, as reflected on by Mitsui Mariko (see Chapter 6), now means that, in the second decade of the twenty-first century, Japanese women find themselves immiserated at home and sexualised abroad (see Morita). In this concluding chapter we reflect on the fact this decades-long decline in the social status of Japanese women has largely escaped the notice of the global sisterhood.[2]

---

[1] While Takasato Suzuyo and the late Matsui Yayori were engaged from the 1980s with feminists in the English-speaking world and Asia, translations of Japanese-language feminist writings declined in subsequent decades, as did, to our knowledge, speaking invitations extended to Japanese feminists to attend conferences in English-speaking countries; notwithstanding sustained engagement by South Korean feminists with Japanese sisters over the 'comfort women' issue.

[2] The 2021 World Economic Forum *Global Gender Gap Report* (2021 37) does note wide disparities in economic power and political representation between Japanese men and women, but emphasises improvement in these indicators, and highlights, oddly,

For its part, Japan's feminist movement in recent years has attempted to strengthen itself through drawing inspiration and practical knowledge from its South Korean counterpart. As will be described, this has led to interaction and exchange between feminist organisations in the two countries, the translation of feminist books,[3] and the adoption in Japan of South Korean organising techniques like those successfully deployed by activists in support of the 'comfort women'. As Yang Ching-Ja narrates in Chapter 7, South Korean and Japan-based feminists have a long history of this kind of collaboration, but in the past it has been more likely for Japan-resident '*zainichi*' feminist groups than others (see Norma, 'Abolitionism in the History of the Transnational "Justice for Comfort Women" Movement in Japan and South Korea'). Now though, more than ethnicity, feminist collaboration across the two countries tends to occur on the basis of political and ideological alignment. At the same time, this collaboration has practical orientation: Japanese feminists are aware of the achievements of their Korean sisters, and learn from their tactics in hopes of bringing about similar social change in Japan.[4]

---

the closing of 'gender gaps' in primary, secondary, and tertiary education in Japan, despite entrenched problems in female admission to science and technology degrees. Japan's continuing low ranking in the 'gender gap' index does not prompt bodies like UN Women to propose an agenda for intervention, even if the Committee on the Elimination of Discrimination Against Women's 2016 country report on Japan does stress, in the strongest terms, the Committee's objection to Japan's judiciary declaring the Convention inapplicable in the country. See https://docstore.ohchr.org/SelfServices/FilesHandler.ashx?enc=6QkG1d%2fPPRiCAqhKb7yhsryr9E9fM8JLxSfpAS5QTBCjaoYUCJTappT6L0KnewZnWVtHe85eNjSs33vAagefQMojwEB%2f0mSHGEkj2WYIs2kuml9qwmUZnNdqQkb1cMZI16gizPN8S1VBWtEgpQvFYQ%3d%3d. The United Nations Department of Economic and Social Affairs *The World's Women* 2020 report highlights women's employment in non-regular work in Japan as causing the large wage gap, but does not quantify the proportion of national income accruing to female citizens. This figure would likely be shocking, and convey more accurately the immiseration of the Japanese female population, as well as the power wielded over them by men who can collectively draw on far greater resources.

[3] Korean feminist literature, like Han Kang's *Vegetarian*, which was published in Japanese in 2011, and *Kim Jiyoung, Born 1982*, published in Japanese in 2018, circulated at a time when learning Korean language became a popular pastime among young Japanese women.

[4] For example, staff at People Against Pornography and Sexual Violence (PAPS) collaborates with the Korea Cyber Sexual Violence Response Center over approaches to removal of 'revenge' pornography and other materials. The South Korean government supports this activity, while PAPS must independently respond to a constant flood of requests from

The achievements of Korean feminists are unmistakeable, and have attracted global attention over the last 5 years, not least from Japanese feminists. Developments in feminist organising occurred in South Korea earlier than in western countries where the so-called #MeToo movement arose in 2017. In South Korea, young women mobilised online from 2015, and, already by 2017, feminist book sales had expanded 6 times (Lee 7). In early 2016, major street vigils of women outside Gangnam station protested a murder in the area (Izaakson and Kim), and in 2018, a series of women-only rallies, attracting 100,000 participants in total, were held in Seoul's main square to protest spy-cam filming crimes, abortion restrictions, and to promote anti-beauty ideology among women (Kuk et al.). The anti-beauty movement continues today among women in South Korea (Park), and has caused declines in revenues for the country's cosmetics and fashion industries. Years of feminist campaigning against a website hosting user-uploaded pornography (e.g., spy-cam and 'revenge' pornography) called Sora.net resulted in the arrest of its owners in 2018 (Jeong), and in 2020, a raft of laws against online sex crimes and digital grooming were enacted (Kan), and South Korea's sexual age-of-consent was lifted from 13 to 16 years. An even bigger investigation by feminists over two years led, in 2020, to the arrest of men running an online subscriber pornography forum. This so-called 'nth-room' case involved the blackmail, extortion, rape, and self-harm of over 100 women and underage girls orchestrated by men operating an online network for sixty thousand subscribers. Feminist agitation was behind the case coming to light, as well as, later, the South Korean government investigating and publicly releasing the names of subscribers. Two of the male organisers are now serving sentences each longer than 30 years. While the election of a left-wing government in South Korea in 2017 aided feminists in these achievements, the scale and intensity of feminist mobilisation in the country, which continues today, was greeted by Japanese activists with wonderment, even if some were mystified by its causes and puzzled at its radicalism.[5]

victims in Japan who are individually harmed by pornography circulating online either produced through the sex industry, or through spy-cam crimes, or by former partners.

[5] Some Japanese feminists are, further, hostile to the radicalism of South Korean feminism, including some '*zainichi*' feminist groups. Their perspective saw the translation into Japanese in 2021 of a book critical of the South Korean movement (Kim Lee and Shin).

South Korean feminists had been active before 2015 in a more limited way organising against the country's sex industry. As Yang Ching-Ja describes in Chapter 7, in 2018 and before, Japanese feminists like Kitahara Minori participated in tours to South Korea as part of fundraising efforts for the launch of the War and Women's Human Rights Museum in Seoul. These tours incorporated visits to South Korean feminist organisations, including those overseeing support services for survivors of the sex industry, such as the Salim Center in Pusan. These organisations, which had by then operated for 2 decades, promote an understanding of prostitution as a form of violence against women, and were the political force behind the enactment of South Korea's legislation in 2004 that suppresses most of the sex industry's activities in the country and its customers (see Norma, 'Australia and South Korea: A Country Promoting Sex Exploitation and a Country Combating It'). Early on, Fujiwara Shihoko from the now-defunct Lighthouse travelled repeatedly to meet with them, and following that, members of PAPS, Colabo, and the Violence Against Women in War Research Action Center (VAWW-RAC). As a direct result of this interaction with South Korean anti-prostitution feminists, a coalition was formed in Tokyo in 2019 that aims for similar anti-prostitution laws in Japan, and this group, *Han-Sei-Sakushu Kenkyū Kai* (anti sexual exploitation network in Japan), in 2019, invited activistsJeong Mirye, Byun Jeonghee, and Shin-Pak Jinyoung, as well as members of the prostitution survivors group Taegu Mungchi, to speak in Tokyo. The same group, in late 2019, invited Chung-Ang University's Lee Na-Young to speak both in Osaka and Tokyo on developments in feminist action against South Korea's sex industry, including digital sex crimes and pornography. Lee shortly after assumed directorship of the Korean Council.

As a result, the feminist anti-prostitution perspective that developed in South Korea over 2 decades now influences portions of Japan's civil society, and has produced outcomes like the probable closure of a red-light district in Hyogo prefecture (final decision pending), and the government's refusal in 2020 to issue pandemic relief funds to the sex industry. While strong anti-prostitution movements exist in other countries that have legislation similar to that enacted in South Korea (i.e., Sweden, Norway, Iceland, Canada, France, Ireland, Northern Ireland, Israel, and the US state of Hawaii), it has been South Korean feminism that has been the vehicle of transmission of such ideas into Japan.[6] In fact, the absence of engagement and intervention by feminists from those other countries has been conspicuous. The 2015 visit to Japan of the United Nations Special Rapporteur on the Sale of Children, Child Prostitution and Child Pornography caused uproar in the country among right-wing online groups (see Ministry of Foreign Affairs of Japan); foreign fathers' rights groups organise locally in Japan (Sim), and local universities host foreign academic staff openly professing pro-pornography views. In other words, the lacuna created in twenty-first-century Japan by the failure of the global sisterhood to sufficiently support a wide range of local feminist efforts creates opportunities for reactionary, anti-feminist forces to proliferate,[7] whether these forces are led by men locally or from abroad.

Feminist Knowledge Transfer

Collaboration between the Japanese and South Korean feminist movements now takes place over a range of issues more varied than those of prostitution and the 'comfort women'. Crucial to this broadened engagement with South Korean feminism was the launch in 2021 of Ajuma Books by Kitahara Minori through her business Love Piece Club (see Chapter 2). The organisational epitaph of this publishing house reads in part:

> Ajuma Books is a sisterhood publishing company. The word 'ajuma' in Korean refers, in beautiful terms, to women who are middle-aged and older. We launched Ajuma Books in the hope of giving voice to lots of ajuma (and future ajuma!)…Let's build the global sisterhood together.

---

[6] For example, none of the major feminist anti-prostitution books that circulate in English-speaking countries are translated into Japanese, and none of the proponents of the movement, except for Catharine MacKinnon, have spoken in the country.

[7] This failure is perhaps elucidated through comparison with the Okinawan struggle against US military bases. Foreign engagement in the form of scholarship, documentaries, participation in protest groups, translation, lobbying, and activist tours has been consistent, thorough, and far-reaching over the last 20 years. From our survey of the English-language scholarly literature, no similar foreign involvement in Japan's feminist movement is recorded, even if there are exceptions among Japanese women working in universities abroad.

Ajuma Books has to date released 3 Korean feminist books in Japanese translation. Two of them, both published in 2021, address contemporary South Korean feminist organising, and Kitahara Minori, in her introduction to one, suggests that 'South Korean feminists, with their bodies on the line, teach us to dispense with upstanding forms of feminism that are pursued with smiles and velvet gloves, and instead to take up the weapon of verbal invective and abuse, and wield it to the best possible effect' (Chon 375). She praises their rhetorical 'mirroring' techniques that aim to raise political consciousness among women online about the way men see and talk about them. (For example, feminists customarily greeting each other with the word 'hayongga', which is the phrase Korean men online use to solicit girls for prostitution.) Kitahara Minori thinks this approach succeeds in neutralising the woman-hating of the online environment, and has empowered South Korean feminists to prosecute their own political movement without regard to what male detractors say and do. The '4B' movement that grew out of this online feminist activity, which involves women boycotting marriage, childbirth, romance, and sexual relationships (Lee and Jeong), arose out of the online community of women who forged the 'mirroring' strategy (see Do-own Kim). The strategy is credited with training women to overcome social inhibition to the extent they are able to challenge institutions like marriage and childbirth. This strategy of the Korean feminist movement is relevant to the problem, discussed in the Introduction to this book, that feminists see as behind the failure of the #MeToo campaign in Japan. Social pressure generated by high-profile men publicly attacking survivors and other women speaking out[8] is seen by Japanese feminists as having produced a downwardly spiralling situation in which the declining numbers of women speaking out make attacks on those who do more likely. Kitahara believes that, compared to South Korea, nowadays 'Japan must look quite the feminist wasteland, after having turned its back on survivors of sexual violence for so long [i.e., including 30 years of denying the claims of the 'comfort women']' (Chon 377). Kitahara reflects on the aim of South Korea's feminist movement not to change men but to support women

---

[8] An example of this is former Minister for Finance Aso Taro's comment about a sexually harassed woman journalist being a 'honeytrap' to snare scandalous news stories, and remarking that if news outlets wanted to avoid the sexual harassment of their employees, they ought to deploy male journalists ('Seifu Kōkan No Bankisha Wa Dansei Nomi "Datō Denai" Seifu Tōbensho').

to change themselves. This 'support' does not take any form of liberal empowerment. Rather, South Korean feminists 'teach women what it means to be a woman in a society that hates you' (Chon 332). Through this teaching it is envisaged that women will become enamoured to criticism and sanction, and come to see their comprehensive victimhood as a position from which no act of resistance can be wrongfooted or excessive.

This spirit of disregard for male opinion drove the development of South Korea's anti-beauty, post-femininity '*tal-corset*' movement, referred to as '*datsu-koru*' (literally, 'removing the corset') in Japanese, which is widely discussed by Japanese feminists, even if none of its ideas or practices yet circulate in the country. The decision, nonetheless, of Keio University Press to publish a Japanese translation in 2022 of the book *Beauty and Misogyny* by English radical feminist theorist Sheila Jeffreys follows its release in Korean in 2018 by the publisher Yeolda Books. In other words, not only are Korean feminist books increasingly translated into Japanese, the translation decisions of South Korean feminist publishers, like If Books and Yeolda Books, are followed by Japanese counterparts. One of the chapters in the second South Korean book released by Ajuma Books in 2021, *Ne no Nai Feminizumu* (*Rootless Feminism*), was written by Kuk Jihye who is the founder of Yeolda Books. Yeolda Books has released translations of English-language radical feminist theory books, including by Sheila Jeffreys, Dee Graham, and Gail Dines. Kuk spoke about some of their ideas at Doshisha University in 2019, and her future influence on Japan's feminist movement is potentially significant for the radicalism of the ideas that will enter the country from the English-speaking world.

Inspiration for feminist campaigning and practical knowledge of its conduct is already drawn by Japanese feminists from major South Korean campaigns. For example, Kitahara Minori recalls being motivated to create the 'Flower demo' project after witnessing the enormous 2016–2017 Candlelight Democracy rallies against President Park Geun-Hye, as well as the weekly 'Wednesday protests' staged since January 1992 by 'comfort women' survivors and their supporters outside the Japanese embassy in Seoul. Nitō Yumeno, too, notes that Colabo's successful 'I Was Bought' travelling photograph exhibition was originally inspired by similar initiatives pursued by 'comfort women' survivors in South Korea. In practical matters of fundraising for political campaigning, Yang Ching-Ja's organisation *Kibōtane* sponsors the Japan-branch of the Marymond social enterprise that successfully raises funds for advocacy in support of the 'comfort women' survivors in South Korea through consumer goods branded with flower designs chosen by survivors (https://www.marymond.jp/). In conjunction with *Kibōtane's* projects sponsoring the travel of Japanese youth to South Korea to interact with counterparts similarly involved in the 'comfort women' issue (see Chapter 7), the enterprise links the organisation to different parts of South Korea's civil sector.

A WORLD OF DIFFERENCE

Japanese feminists often attribute the success of the South Korean feminist movement compared to Japan to, as Yang Ching-Ja's comments in Chapter 7 reflect, superior political education and activist technique forged through South Korea's Democratic Revolution of 1987. When applied to younger generations of feminists, this explanation nominates either the 2017 Candlelight Revolution or the 2015 stepped-up campaign in support of 'comfort women' survivors as having had the same effect. These explanations of South Korea's relative progress in women's rights do not reflect, however, differences in social organisation between the two countries. While, certainly, the rise to power of a left-wing government in 2017 was a boost to local feminism (in contrast to Japan's continuation under right-wing rule), there are differences affecting the condition of women in the respective countries that are even more entrenched than party politics. The first is the development, from the 1960s, of a large sex industry in Japan trading women and children both for prostitution as well as pornography production. South Korea, too, did have a large prostitution sector up until the passing of an anti-prostitution law in 2004 (from which time the industry's size froze or slightly declined). But in Japan, even more seriously, possessing child pornography was not defined as a crime until 2014, and the trading of child pornography was fully deregulated up to 1999.[9] The pornography industry operated under almost no restriction until 2016, and its commercial operations extended even to Taiwan.

In her introduction to the above-mentioned Ajuma Books-published *Hayonga* (2021), Kitahara Minori reflects on this fundamental difference between Japan and South Korea. She reminds readers, correctly, that a

---

[9] As a result, bricks-and-mortar shops selling child pornography openly operated in inner-city Kabukicho in the 1990s. Even today, shops selling footage of barely clothed children mimicking sexual poses openly operate in Akihabara.

pornography industry does not exist in South Korea, and that Japan is in fact the only country in Asia that permits the operation of a legalised pornography industry within its borders (Chon 376). She calls Japan's pornography market a large-scale, legalised, sophisticated version of the South Korean 'nth-room' business, which, as described, shook the foundations of that country in 2020. In Japan, in contrast, Kitahara writes, lines are wholly blurred between sexual violence and the commercial world, and it is not uncommon for the sex industry to be defended as a legitimate social safety net for women in the country, as alluded to in Nitō's discussion of the ways in which men approach girls on the street offering 'help' (see Chapter 4).[10] While the 'nth-room' case attracted a great deal of attention worldwide, equally heinous cases when they occur in Japan do not make international headlines. Japanese feminists simply do not yet have the organising power to agitate over issues of sexual exploitation to produce results like that generated by the South Korean feminist movement.

Illustrating this weakness were events occurring in the lead-up to the Tokyo Olympics held in 2021. Even though the eyes of the world were on this event for a number of years, the desperate efforts of the Japanese Olympic Committee from 2020 attempting to prevent spy-cam filming of female athletes went largely unnoticed outside of Japan. After receiving complaints from local female track athletes, the Committee came to realise that Japan's legal environment incorporated no mechanism to intervene in the sexualised filming and photographing of Olympic delegates, even those underage, and that such materials would be uploaded to the internet, often for profit ('Seiteki Gazō No Tsūhō 2500ken Gorin Mae Kara Baizō, Tokutei Saito'). The Committee frantically canvased possibilities for various legal and technological measures to be taken ('"Tōsatsu, Seiteki Gazō Higai Kara Asuriito Wo Mamoru - Genjō to Kadai" Wo Tēma Toshite Shimpojiumu Ga Kaisai Saremashita'), and even made reports to police of materials it had found of athletes circulating online. The Committee's frequent appeals for legal measures to be established before the Olympics were regularly reported in the Japanese-language media, but foreign media likely overlooked this relatively unusual spectacle of a high-level national body concerning itself with spy-cam filming problems because feminist campaigning hadn't sufficiently brought the

---

[10] This opinion is, indeed, commonly heard, and even from high-profile 'progressive' male commentators in Japan such as Miyadai Shinji.

seriousness of the problem, and its implications for overseas female athletes, to public attention. Even worse than South Korea, in Japan the 'spy-cam' genre is a historically developed and profitable sector of Japan's legally operating pornography industry.[11] The ubiquity of the spy-cam filming of women in Japanese society (including via drones dispatched over outdoor hot springs baths) is now driven by the incomes men receive through uploading these materials to websites that are almost wholly unregulated (Chifumi). Different from South Korea, spy-cam, upskirting, and deep-fake footage circulates not just through secure subscriber-based sites like the South Korean Sora.net, but openly as a 'genre' of pornography that is even sold in brick-and-mortar shops ('Tōsatsu No Yami 2 "Kane Ni Naru Eizō" DVD Hanbai, Yūryō Haishin Mo'). While South Korean women, too, suffer the threat of public filming, Kitahara Minori sees this environment in Japan as producing a problem of wholly different magnitude for women and children who are victimised on the basis of consumer demand generated by customers of a normalised and legalised pornography industry. Further, the prevalence and drivers of spy-cam filming go unrecognised and unacknowledged in Japan because no '*molka*' anti-spy-cam feminist campaign has yet arisen in the country similar to the one that brought the problem to public attention in South Korea (and, indeed, the world) (see, for example, Taylor).

Conclusion

The modest and limited feminist movement that this book captures through the testimonies of 6 contemporary Japanese activists is nonetheless a valuable record of the efforts and achievements of the individual women themselves, often pursued in hostile,unyielding,and personally harrowing circumstances over many years and decades. There is certainly nothing modest nor limited about the achievements of these 6 women over their lives. The feminist movement they contribute to, however, does not yet achieve enough influence or reach to prevent substantial social decline among Japanese women and girls in the twenty-first century. This

---

[11] Over the years 2005 and 2006, the Anti-Pornography and Prostitution Research Group (APP) undertook ground-level surveys of hotels, bathhouses, and other public venues in Japan likely to attract spy-cam filming, and found that business proprietors were surprisingly aware of the problem due to their own experiences of encountering perpetrators in their facilities.

is not, as has been made clear, the fault of the feminist movement, and there are other countries in the world—perhaps Iran, Russia, Afghanistan, India, and Turkey—where similar declines in the position of women have possibly occurred over the same time period. It is significant, though, that the contributors to this book mention in positive terms engagement with feminists overseas, and generally see feminism as an internationalist movement that profits from connections between women in the form of 'global sisterhood'. Yamamoto Jun (Chapter 3), Nitō Yumeno (Chapter 4), Mitsui Mariko (Chapter 6), and Yang Ching-Ja (Chapter 7) all mention having gained inspiration or insight from contact with activists abroad. In spite of this, the Japanese feminist movement in the twenty-first century is neglected by the global sisterhood, even if South Korean sisters maintain strong and varied links. This neglect is only minutely remedied in the current book, but it was compiled in the hope that the English-speaking feminist world might draw inspiration from South Korean sisters in forging closer relationships and ties with Japan's feminist movement. We might feel a sense of obligation to lend this support, given the large contribution of the male English-speaking world to the pornification and trivialisation (as militarists, sex industrialists, and culture industry producers and consumers) of Japanese women, but no such burden of duty need motivate a response. The fact is, as demonstrated across the breadth of testimony in this book, and also in the decades-long experience of its two authors, the movement and its proponents retain experience and knowledge that has beneficial insights for feminist campaigns outside of Japan.[12] Considerations of gain and loss, of course, do not motivate the global sisterhood, and it is rather the insider perspective, and personal touch, of this book's account of Japan's contemporary feminist movement that we hope will move English-speaking sisters to greater acts of solidarity and support.

---

[12] We think specifically of the anti-surrogacy feminist campaign in Japan, which currently succeeds at a time when similar efforts in other countries founder. See the Japan Coalition Against Surrogacy Practices (http://nosurrogacy.lib.i.dendai.ac.jp/jp/).

References

Ampo Japan-Asia Quarterly Review. *Voices from the Japanese Women's Movement*. M.E. Sharpe, 1996.
Ando, Rei. "Domestic Violence and Japan's COVID-19 Pandemic." *Japan Focus*, vol. 18, no. 7, 2020, pp. 1–11.
Beniyama, Ayaka. "Barriers to 'Equal Pay for Work of Equal Value' for Women in Japan: Assessing the Potential for Change." *Journal of Industrial Relations*, vol. 62, no. 4, 2020, pp. 630–50.
Borovoy, Amy Beth. *The Too-Good Wife: Alcohol, Codependency, and the Politics of Nurturance in Postwar Japan*. University of California Press, 2005.
Bulbeck, Chilla. *Sex, Love and Feminism in the Asia Pacific*. Routledge, 2009.
Chifumi, Shinya. "'Upskirt' Problem Intensifies with Easier Access to Spy Cameras." *Asahi Shimbun*, 27 Sept. 2021, https://www.asahi.com/ajw/articles/14436058.
Chon, Migyon. *Hayonga: Hāi, Okodsukai Dēto Shinai?* Translated by Fumiko Oshima, Ajuma Books, 2021.
Committee on the Elimination of Discrimination Against Women. *Concluding Observations on the Combined Seventh and Eighth Periodic Reports of Japan*. CEDAW/C/JPN/CO/7–8, United Nations, 7 Mar. 2016, https://docstore.ohchr.org/SelfServices/FilesHandler.ashx?enc=6QkGl d%2fPPRiCAq hKb7yhsryr9E9fM8JLxSfpAS5QTBCjaoYUCJTappT6L0KnewZnWVtHe85 eNjSs33vAagefQMojwEB%2f0mSHGEkj2WYIs2kuml9qwmUZnNdqQkb 1cMZI16gizPN8S1VBWtEgpQvFYQ%3d%3d.

Dales, Laura. "Feminist Futures in Japan: Exploring the Work of Haruka Yoko and Kitahara Minori." *Genders, Transgenders and Sexualities in Japan*, edited by Mark McLelland and Romit Dasgupta, Routledge, 2005, pp. 183–89.
———. *Feminist Movements in Contemporary Japan*. Routledge, 2009.
Dalton, Emma. *Sexual Harassment in Japanese Politics*. Palgrave Macmillan, 2021.
Doering, Keiko, et al. "Japanese Women's Experiences of Pharmacological Pain Relief in New Zealand." *Women and Birth*, vol. 27, no. 2, 2014, pp. 121–25.
Do-own Kim, Donna. "Mirroring the Misogynistic Wor(l)d: Civic Imagination and Speech Mirroring Strategy in Korea's Online Feminist Movement." *Popular Culture and the Civic Imagination*, edited by Henry Jenkins et al., New York University Press, 2021, pp. 152–61.
Eckersall, Peter. "The Emotional Geography of Shinjuku: The Case of Chikatetsu Hiroba (Underground Plaza, 1970)." *Japanese Studies*, vol. 31, no. 3, 2011, pp. 333–43.
Fujimura-Fanselow, Kumiko, editor. *Transforming Japan: How Feminism and Diversity Are Making a Difference*. 2011.
Fujita, Takanori. *Korona Hinkon: Zetsubōteki Kakusa Shakai No Shūrai*. Mainichi Shimbun Shuppan, 2021.
Global Gender Gap Report 2021. World Economic Forum, 2021, https://www3.weforum.org/docs/WEF_GGGR_2021.pdf.
Gōdō Shuppan, editor. *Watashi Wa Damaranai: Seibōryoku Wo Nakusu 30 No Shiten*. Gōdō Shuppan, 2021.
Hamada, Iori. "The Kaji-Hara (Housework Harassment) Debates: The Gendering of Housework in Contemporary Japan." *Japan Forum*, vol. 33, no. 4, 2021, pp. 580–607.
Hashimoto, Kenji. "Atarashī Kaikyū Shakai to Josei Rōdō." *The Bulletin of the Society for the Study of Working Women*, no. 63, 2019, pp. 7–28.
Hasunuma, Linda, and Ki-young Shin. "#MeToo in Japan and South Korea: #WeToo, #WithYou." *Journal of Women, Politics & Policy*, vol. 40, no. 1, 2019, pp. 97–111.
"Hirogaru Furawā Demo." *Shimbun Akahata*, 6 Oct. 2019.
Itō, Shiori. *Black Box*. Bungei Shunju, 2017.
Izaakson, Jen, and Tae Kyung Kim. "The South Korean Women's Movement: 'We Are Not Flowers, We Are a Fire.'" *Feminist Current*, June 2020, https://www.feministcurrent.com/2020/06/15/the-south-korean-womens-movement-we-are-not-flowers-we-are-a-fire/.
Japan Communist Party. *Furawā Demo Kara Ichinen Ima Kangaeru Shingata Korona to Jendā*. 2020, https://www.youtube.com/watch?v=VxUaYkIZY3g&list=PL3M7AtnZgh3WwG4I_WgdyBproXgNk428C&index=15.

Jeong, Euisol. *Troll Feminism: The Rise of Popular Feminism in South Korea*. University of York, 2020, https://etheses.whiterose.ac.uk/28959/1/Jeong_203045590.pdf.
Jørgensen, Nina H. B., and Regina E. Rauxloh. "Profiting from Sexual Violence in Armed Conflict: A Case for the Resurrection of the Crime of Enforced Prostitution." *Chinese Journal of International Law*, vol. 19, no. 3, 2020, pp. 393–423, https://doi.org/10.1093/chinesejil/jmaa029.
"Josei No Seikatsu Konkyū Wa 'Sengo Saiaku' 70-Nen Ijō Shien Shitekita Shiga/Otsu-Shi No Shien Dantai Ga Tsutaetai Koto." *NHK*, 13 Dec. 2021, https://www.nhk.or.jp/gendai/comment/0020/topic039.html.
Kan, Hyeong-woo. "Tighter Regulations on Digital Sex Crime Take Effect." *The Korea Herald*, 23 Sept. 2021, http://www.koreaherald.com/view.php?ud=20210923000656.
Kanai, Yoshiko. "Issues for Japanese Feminism." *Voices from the Japanese Women's Movement*, edited by Ampo Japan-Asia Quarterly Review, M.E. Sharpe, 1996, pp. 3–22.
Kano, Ayako. "Backlash, Fight Back, and Back-Pedalling: Responses to State Feminism in Contemporary Japan." *International Journal of Asian Studies*, vol. 8, no. 1, 2011, pp. 41–62.
———. *Japanese Feminist Debates: A Century of Contention on Sex, Love, and Labor*. University of Hawai'i Press, 2016.
Kawata, Fumiko. *Onna Tachi No Komoriuta*. Daisanbumei-sha, 1982.
Kaya, Emiko. "Mitsui Mariko: An Avowed Feminist Assemblywoman." *Japanese Women: New Feminist Perspectives on the Past, Present and Future*, edited by Kumiko Fujimura-Fanselow and Atsuko Kameda, The Feminist Press at the City University of New York, 1995, pp. 384–92.
Kim Lee, Iseul, and Ki-young Shin. *#MeToo No Seijigaku: Koria Feminizumu No Saizensen*. Otsuki Shoten, 2021.
Kitahara, Minori. *Busu No Hirakinaori*. Canaria Communications, 2004.
———. "Hajimatta Furawā Demo." *Watashi Wa Damaranai: Seibōryoku Wo Nakusu 30 No Shiten*, Gōdō Shuppan, pp. 21–24.
———. "Konbini Kara Onna No Ero Hon Ga Nakunatta Hi." *Konbini Kara Ero Hon Ga Nakunaru Hi*, edited by Eiko Tabusa, etc. books, 2019, pp. 20–23.
———. "Manatsu No Kankoku de Hirogatta Hito No Wa." *AERAdot*, Aug. 2019, https://dot.asahi.com/wa/2019082900016.html?page=2.
———, editor. *Nihon No Feminizumu since 1886*. Kawade Shobo Shinsha, 2017.
———. "Sei No Jiko Kettei o Meguru 80nen Dai No Tatakai." *Nihon No Feminizumu since 1886 (Japanese Feminism since 1886)*, edited by Kitahara Minori, Kawade Shobo Shinsha, 2017, pp. 66–71.
———. "Seihigai Wo Kokuso Shita Moto Kusatsu Chōgi No Josei Ga Kaiken: Kaijō No Kanshin to #MeToo No Zure Ni Shōgeki Wo Uketa." *AERAdot*,

15 Dec. 2021, https://news.yahoo.co.jp/articles/36843f4c8294ccb430cba bef5850528ce07e2cff?page=3.
Kitahara, Minori, and Suni Park. *Okusama Wa Aikoku*. Kawade Shobo Shinsha, 2014.
Kitahara, Minori, and Masaru Satō. *Sei to Kokka*. Kawade Shobo Shinsha, 2016.
Kobayashi, Yoshiaki. *A Path Toward Gender Equality: State Feminism in Japan*. Routledge, 2004.
Koch, Gabriele. *Healing Labor: Japanese Sex Work in the Gendered Economy*. Stanford University Press, 2020.
Kuk, Jihye, et al. "Radical Feminism Paves the Way for a Resurgent South Korean Women's Movement." *Feminist Current*, Nov. 2018, https://www.feministcurrent.com/2018/11/07/radical-feminism-paves-way-resurgent-south-korean-womens-movement/?fbclid=IwAR1N8PvxIccL3hK8ivT8eDOConXe1II6BpO6lxd_vtJ6Nxx-Lqrn6-3RtXw.
Lee, Jieun, and Euisol Jeong. "The 4B Movement: Envisioning a Feminist Future with/in a Non-reproductive Future in Korea." *Journal of Gender Studies*, vol. 30, no. 5, July 2021, pp. 633–44.
Lee, Wonyun. *Responding to Misogyny, Reciprocating Hate Speech—South Korea's Online Feminism Movement: Megalia*. Harvard University, 2019, https://dash.harvard.edu/handle/1/37366046.
Lehtonen, Lasse. "Japanese Women Singer-Songwriters of the 1970s: Female Agency, Musical Impact and Social Change." *Popular Music*, vol. 40, no. 1, 2021, pp. 114–38.
Mackie, Vera. *Feminism in Modern Japan*. Routledge Curzon, 2003.
MacKinnon, Catharine. *Butterfly Politics: Changing the World for Women, With a New Preface*. Belknap Press, 2019.
Makino, Masako. *Chikan to Wa Nani Ka: Higai to Enzai Wo Meguru Shakaigaku*. etc. books, 2019.
McMorran, Mark. "Liberating Work in the Tourist Industry." *Rethinking Japanese Feminisms*, edited by Julia Bullock et al. University of Hawai'i Press, 2018, pp. 119–30.
Mies, Maria. *Patriarchy and Accumulation on a World Scale: Women in the International Division of Labour*. Zed Books, 1999.
Ministry of Foreign Affairs of Japan. "Reply from the Special Rapporteur on the Sale of Children, Child Prostitution and Child Pornography." *Press Releases*, https://www.mofa.go.jp/press/release/press4e_000915.html.
Mitsui, Mariko. *Sekuhara 110 Ban*. Shueisha, 1994.
Mitsui, Mariko, and Mutsuko Asakura. *Bakkurasshu No Ikinie: Feminisuto Kanchō Kaikō Jiken*. Junposha, 2012.
Miura, Mari. "Nihon No Feminizumu: Josei Tachi No Undō o Furikaeru." *Nihon No Feminizumu Since 1886*, edited by Kitahara Minori, Kawade Shobo Shinsha, 2019, pp. 8–18.

Morita, Seiya. *Marukusu Shugi, Feminizumu, Sekkusu Wāku Ron*. Keio University Press, 2021.

Muta, Kazue. "Hataraku Ba No Kenryoku Kōzō to Sekushuaru Harasumento: SH Wo Fukashika Sareru Nihon No Tokusei." *The Bulletin of the Society for the Study of Working Women*, no. 63, 2019, pp. 29–42.

Nae, Niculina. "Domestic Vs. Public Power: Japanese Women Three Decades After Equal Employment Opportunity Law." *Euromentor Journal*, vol. 9, no. 3, 2018, pp. 41–54.

Nakagawa, Toshiko. "'Wakariyasui Teki Wa Inai. Kaetai No Wa Josei Ken'o' Furawa Demo Ga Mezasu Mono to Wa, Kitahara." *Mainichi Shimbun*, 28 Feb. 2020, https://mainichi.jp/articles/20200227/k00/00m/040/270000c?_ga=2.101531393.187801529.1583052877-1143210393.158163 8193.

Nakayama, Masahiko, translator. *Uttaeru Onnatachi: Reipu Saiban No Kiroku*. Kodansha, 1979.

Nemoto, Kumiko. "Why Women Won't Wed." *Beyond the Gender Gap in Japan*, edited by Gill Steel, University of Michigan Press, 2019, pp. 67–82.

Nishimura, Junko. *Motherhood and Work in Contemporary Japan*. Routledge, 2016.

Nitō, Yumeno. "Gyakutai, Hinkon, Seibōryoku: Yoru No Machi Wo Samayō Shōjo Wo Sasaeru Mitsu No Katsudō." *Gendai Bijinesu*, 11 Nov. 2017, https://gendai.ismedia.jp/articles/-/53437.

———. *Joshi Kōsei No Ura Shakai*. Kobun, 2014.

———. *Nanmin Kōkōsei: Zetsubō Shakai Wo Ikinuku Watashitachi No Riaru*. Eiji Press, 2013.

Norma, Caroline. "Abolitionism in the History of the Transnational 'Justice for Comfort Women' Movement in Japan and South Korea." *Remembering the Second World War*, edited by Patrick Finney, Routledge, 2017, pp. 115–39.

———. "Australia and South Korea: A Country Promoting Sex Exploitation and a Country Combating It." *Anti Pornography and Prostitution Research Group*, 8 Aug. 2020, https://appinternational.org/2020/08/08/australia-and-south-korea/.

———. *Comfort Women and Post-occupation Corporate Japan*. Routledge, 2018.

———. "FiLiA." *Japan's Sex Industry in the Year of Corona, 2020*, 19 Nov. 2020, https://filia.org.uk/latest-news/2020/11/19/japans-sex-industry-in-the-year-of-corona-2020.

———. "The First #MeToo Activists." *CrossCurrents*, vol. 69, no. 4, 2019, pp. 439–61.

———. "The Geisha-Effect: Western Capitalisation on Japanese Commercial Sexual Exploitation." *Anti Pornography and Prostitution Research Group*, 23 May 2021, https://appinternational.org/2021/05/23/geisha_effect/.

Norma, Caroline, and Emma Dalton. "Big Time Misogyny in Small-Town Japan." *Anti-Pornography-and-Prostitution Research Group (APP)*, 2020, https://appinternational.org/2020/11/29/big_time_misogyny_in_s mall_town_japan/.

Norma, Caroline, and Seiya Morita. "Feminist Action Against Pornography in Japan: Unexpected Success in an Unlikely Place." *Dignity: A Journal on Sexual Exploitation and Violence*, vol. 4, no. 4, 2020, pp. 1–24.

Ogasawara, Yuko. *Office Ladies and Salaried Men: Power, Gender and Work in Japanese Companies*. University of California Press, 1998.

Oshima, Fumiko, translator. *Ne No Nai Feminizumu: Femisaido Ni Tachimukatta Megariatachi*. Ajuma Books, 2021.

Otsuka, Kahoru. *Report on the Lecture in Commemoration of Receipt of the Order of Merit of the Kingdom of Norway at Iidabashi Volunteer Center*. 23 Sept. 2021, https://frihet.exblog.jp/32314925/.

Park, Hyejung. "Throwing Off the Corset: A Contemporary History of the Beauty Resistance Movement in South Korea." *Dignity: A Journal on Sexual Exploitation and Violence*, vol. 5, Dec. 2020.

Pateman, Carole. *The Sexual Contract*. Stanford University Press, 2018.

Science Council of Japan. '*Dōi No Umu' Wo Chūkaku ni Oku Keihō Kaisei Ni Mukete: Seibōryoku Ni Tai Suru Kokusai Jinken Kijun No Han'ei*. Science Council of Japan, 29 Sept. 2020, https://www.scj.go.jp/ja/info/kohyo/pdf/kohyo-24-t298-5.pdf.

"Seifu Kōkan No Bankisha Wa Dansei Nomi 'Datō Denai' Seifu Tōbensho." *Asahi Shimbun*, 27 Apr. 2018.

"Seiteki Gazō No Tsūhō 2500ken Gorin Mae Kara Baizō, Tokutei Saito." *Nihon Nikkei Shimbun*, 17 Oct. 2021, https://www.nikkei.com/article/DGXZQO UE163GB0W1A011C2000000/.

Seo, Akwi. "Korean Women's Redress Movement for 'Comfort Women.'" *Rethinking Japanese Feminisms*, edited by Julia Bullock et al., University of Hawai'i Press, 2018, pp. 230–50.

Shibahara, Taeko. *Japanese Women and the Transnational Feminist Movement Before World War II*. Temple University Press, 2014.

Shin, Ki-young. "Seika Sareta Kenryoku—#MeToo Undō Ga Akiraka Ni Shita Harasumento No Jittai to Henkaku No Kanōsei." *The Bulletin of the Society for the Study of Working Women*, no. 63, 2019, pp. 43–65.

Sim, Walter. "Japan-Based French Father on Hunger Strike Against 'Child Abduction' as Olympics Open." *The Straits Times*, 24 July 2021, https://www.straitstimes.com/asia/east-asia/japan-based-french-father-on-hunger-str ike-against-child-abduction-as-olympics-open.

Siripala, Thisanka. "Japan's Same Surname Law for Married Couples Is in the Hands of the Diet." *Diplomat*, 8 July 2021, https://thediplomat.com/2021/07/japans-same-surname-law-for-married-couples-is-in-the-hands-of-the-diet/.

Stalker, Nancy. "Flower Empowerment: Rethinking Japan's Traditional Art as Women's Labor." *Rethinking Japanese Feminisms*, University of Hawai'i Press, 2018, pp. 103–18.

Steel, Gill. "Introduction." *Beyond the Gender Gap in Japan*, edited by Gill Steel, University of Michigan Press, 2019, pp. 1–17.

Suzuki, Makoto. "Rikōkei Bunya No Jendā Gyappu Kaishō No Tame 'Nyūshi Kuōta-Sei' No Giron Wo." *FNN Puraimu Onrain*, 27 Dec. 2021, https://www.fnn.jp/articles/-/291370?display=full.

Tai, Eika. *Comfort Women Activism: Critical Voices from the Perpetrator State*, Hong Kong University Press, 2020.

Taylor, Josh. "South Korea: Woman Reportedly Kills Herself after Being Secretly Filmed by Doctor." *The Guardian*, 2 Oct. 2019, https://www.theguardian.com/world/2019/oct/02/south-korea-woman-kills-herself-after-being-secretly-filmed-by-doctor-reports.

"Tōsatsu No Yami 2 'Kane Ni Naru Eizō' DVD Hanbai, Yūryō Haishin Mo." *Shiga Shimbun*, 27 Dec. 2020, https://www.saga-s.co.jp/articles/-/319493.

"'Tōsatsu, Seiteki Gazō Higai Kara Asurīto Wo Mamoru—Genjō to Kadai' Wo Tēma Toshite Shimpojiumu Ga Kaisai Saremashita." *JSPO Plus*, 9 July 2021, https://media.japan-sports.or.jp/column/61.

Toyama, Kazuhiro. "Tokyo Medical Univ. to Pay $520K to Settle Lawsuit over Entry Exam Rigging." *The Mainichi*, 28 July 2021, https://mainichi.jp/english/articles/20210728/p2a/00m/0na/011000c.

Tsunoda, Yukiko. "Atarashii Yoake Wo Tsugeru Furawādemo." *Furawādemo Wo Kiroku Suru*, edited by Tamaka Ogawa, etc. books, 2020, pp. 26–29.

———. *Sei to Hōritsu*. Iwanami Shinsho, 2013.

———. *Sei to Hōritsugaku*. Yūhikaku, 1991.

Tsunoda, Yukiko, and Kazuko Itō, editors. *Datsu Sekushuaru Harasumento Sengen*. Kamogawa Shuppan, 2021.

Ueno, Chizuko. "Feminisms in Japan since the Second Wave to the Present: Its History and Achievement." *Routledge Handbook of East Asian Gender Studies*, Routledge, 2020, pp. 75–94.

———. "Self-Determination on Sexuality? Commercialization of Sex Among Teenage Girls in Japan." *Inter-Asia Cultural Studies*, vol. 4, no. 2, 2003, pp. 317–24.

WAN Josei Kikin. *Minaosō Keihō Seihanzai*. 2018, https://www.moj.go.jp/content/001316277.pdf.

Welker, James, et al., editors. *Rethinking Japanese Feminisms*. University of Hawai'i Press, 2017.

Xue, Aviva, and Kate Rose. *Weibo Feminism: Expression, Activism, and Social Media in China*. Bloomsbury Publishing, 2022.
Yajima, Daisuke, and Fumio Masutani. "Fukusue Igakubu, Nyūshi De Danjo Ni Sa Wo Settei. Daigaku Mei Wa Meigen Sezu." *Asahi Shinbun*, 12 Oct. 2018, https://www.asahi.com/articles/ASLBD36HFLBDUTIL00M.html.
Yamamoto, Jun. *Jūsansai, 'Watashi' Wo Nakushita Watashi*. Asahi Shimbun Publications, 2017.
Yang, Ching-Ja. "Katarenai Kioku Wo Kiku: 'Ianfu' Sabaibā No Katari." *Seibōryoku Hikai Wo Kiku: "Ianfu" Kara Gendai No Seisakushu e*, edited by Puja Kim and Akane Onozawa, Iwanami Shoten, 2020, pp. 121–42.
———. "Saguru/Fukumeru: Kim Hak-Sun San Kara Hajimatta #MeToo." *Onna Mo Otoko Mo*, vol. 132, 2018, pp. 26–28.
———. "'Seigiren' Basshingu No Kōzu: Hōdō to Jijitsu." *Sekai*, vol. 935, Aug. 2020, pp. 152–58.
———. "Tatakaitsuzukeru Joseitachi: Kankoku Ni Okeru Nihongun 'ianfu' Higaisha to Shiensha No Tsuiseki." *Bauraku Kaihō*, vol. 804, Apr. 2021, pp. 12–20.
Zhou, Yanfei. "How Women Bear the Brunt of COVID-19's Damages on Work." *Japan Labor Issues*, vol. 5, no. 28, 2021, pp. 2–8.

Index

A
Act on Promotion of Gender Equality in the Political Field. *See* candidate gender equality law
advisory council, on sex crimes, 30, 35
Ajuma Books, 18, 114–117
AJWRC. *See* Asia-Japan Women's Resource Center
Akamatsu, Ryōko, 81
Akane, Onozawa, 12, 98
Alliance of Feminist Representatives, 70, 71. *See also* Femigiren
Amour, 20
Anti-Pornography and Prostitution Research Group, 7, 19, 54, 119
anti sexual exploitation network in Japan, 113
APP. *See* Anti-Pornography and Prostitution Research Group
Arai, Shōko, 18, 70, 80
Article 709, 62–65

Asia-Japan Women's Resource Center, 7

B
backlash, 4, 43, 73
  to gender equality, 72, 73, 82
  to Itō Shiori, 33
  See also Japan Conference; Twitter
Basic Law for a Gender Equal Society, 72
Beauty and Misogyny, 116
Busu No Hirakinaori, 18

C
candidate gender equality law, 80, 81
Candlelight Democracy, 116
Candlelight Revolution, 117
CEDAW, 61, 75
chikan, 10, 23. *See also* public molestation
child protection services, 47, 48, 50
children

abused, 29, 47
and poverty, 6
parental access to, 3, 22
rights of, 47, 50
services for, 47
sexual exploitation of, 45
welfare of, 47, 48, 50
Christian Women's Temperance Union. *See Kyōfukai*
Chungok, Yun, 98
Civil Code, 32, 62
Colabo
as an NGO, 17, 40, 41
bus café, 49
collaboration with South Korean organisations, 43
growth of, 40
in the media, 42
kimoi ojisan, 41
teenage girls, 8, 40–43, 51
Tsubomi night café, 48
Twitter, 44
See also 'I Was Bought'; Nitō Yumeno
comfort women
activists, 86–89, 91, 95, 102, 107, 111
advocates, 88, 89
and colonialism, 101
and feminism, 9, 86, 95, 97, 104, 114, 117
and *zainichi*, 86, 98, 99, 101, 111
December 2015 Agreement, 88, 89, 91
Femizemi, 104
in the media, 18, 67, 91, 92
Japanese liberals' lack of support for, 92
Kibōtane, 86, 89, 92, 93, 104, 107, 116, 117
Kim, Hak-Sun, 67, 87, 88, 100, 101

Kitahara Minori's commitment to, 19
Korean Council, 87–90, 92, 106
Marymond, 104, 116
parallel with Flower demo, 106
perception of Japanese youth, 92, 93, 117
public memorials, 88
South Korea-Japan Agreement, 88. *See also* December 2015 Agreement
South Korean Constitutional Court decision, 91
Wednesday protests, 116
Yang Ching-Ja's research on, 86
See also survivor
Committee on the Elimination of Discrimination Against Women, 111
Community Organizing Japan, 31
'compensated dating', 21, 42, 45. *See also enjo kōsai*
convenience stores, 44
and nappies, 21
and pornographic magazines, 20–22
Convention on the Elimination of All Forms of Discrimination against Women, 61
Optional Protocol to, 82
See also CEDAW
court case
2019 sexual assault, 66, 67
Flower demo, 66
Itō, Shiori, 4
Kim, Hak-Sun, 101
sexual harassment, 59, 63
Song Shin-Do, 97
Toyonaka City Council, 81
criminal law, 54, 56, 57, 61, 67. *See also* rape

D

December 2015 Agreement, 88–91
dignity, 64, 73
Doi, Takako, 72, 75
domestic violence, 6, 7, 10
  as a violation of human rights, 44, 67, 101
  in Korean society, 107

E

enjo kōsai, 21, 45. *See also* 'compensated dating'
Equal Employment Opportunity Law, 74, 75, 81
erotica, 21, 22. *See also* pornography

F

Femigiren
  association with *Q no Kai*, 81
  founding of, 79
  gender quotas, 72, 80
  involvement in protests, 80
  See also Alliance of Feminist Representatives
Femin, 97
feminism
  and comfort women, 13, 86, 95, 97, 104, 114, 117
  and women's liberation, 95, 97
  as a 'global sisterhood', 110, 114, 120
  elitism, 96
  global, 13
  housewife, 9
  Japanese, 2, 8, 9, 11, 20, 86, 94, 96, 97, 104, 115
  minority, 10
  radical, 9, 19
  scholarship on, 58
  See also South Korea; women's libber

feminist
  academic, 7, 8, 11, 17, 42, 114
  activist, 2, 7–9, 11, 12, 43, 55, 56, 66, 70, 75, 77, 98, 104, 113, 117, 119, 120
  anti-, 95, 97, 114
  counselling, 28
  grassroots, 2, 7, 8, 12, 13, 54
  mobilisation, 6, 112
  ridicule of, 82
  scholarship, 7, 70
feminist movement
  global, 2, 6, 110
  grassroots, 2, 7, 12, 13, 54
  Japanese, 2, 4, 6, 8, 9, 11, 13, 114, 119, 120
  South Korean, 105, 112, 114, 115, 117, 118
Femizemi, 104
Flower demo
  as place to discuss sexual violence, 25
  effectiveness of, 32
  Itō, Shiori, 16, 18, 33, 104
  Marymond, 104
  media response to, 16, 23
  reason behind, 24, 25
  sex crime acquittals, 16, 23, 32
  See also Candlelight Democracy; Kiatahara, Minori
'4B' movement, 115
Fujiwara Shihoko, 113
Fukuoka
  sexual harassment case, 56, 59

G

geisha, 110
gender inequality, 26, 34, 82
  in education, 74, 75
  in politics, 71
Geun-Hye, Park, 116

Global Gender Gap Index, 33, 65
Group for making our own equal employment opportunity law, 74

H
Hāchū, 17
Han-Sei-Sakushu Kenkyū Kai, 113
Hayongga, 115
Higuchi, Keiko, 74
Hiroshi, Nakasatomi, 20
human rights
  and #MeToo, 23, 25
  and sexual harassment, 64, 68
  international standards, 62, 65
  of children, 47
  women's rights as, 12, 23, 25, 62, 99, 100
Human Rights Now, 65

I
Ichikawa, Fusae, 7, 74
If Books, 116
Igarashi, Megumi, 18
International Labour Organization, 66
International Women's Year Action Group, 70, 74
Ishida, Ikuko, 7, 23
Itō, Kazuko, 54, 56
Itō, Shiori
  and Flower demo, 16, 18, 33, 104
  Black Box, 16
  role in #MeToo movement, 4, 33
  'I Was Bought', 40, 42, 44, 48, 116

J
Japan Conference, 72, 73, 81
Japanese Olympic Committee, 118
jidō sōdanjo. *See* child protection services
Joshi Kōsei no Ura Shakai, 42

journalists, 4, 57, 97
  female, 16, 33, 66, 67, 115
  male, 18, 67, 115
Jūsansai, 'Watashi' wo Nakushita Watashi. *See Losing Myself at Age 13*

K
Kamata, Kanoko, 31
Kamikawa Yōko, 32
Kawata, Fumiko, 87
  and feminism, 95, 96
  and Ueno Chizuko, 95
Keihō Kaisei Shimin Purojekuto, 36
Kibōtane
  and *Femizemi*, 104
  comfort women, 86, 89, 92, 93, 104, 116, 117
  Kitahara, Minori, 104, 105, 116
  leadership of, 86
  Marymond, 104, 116
  online seminars, 104
  'seeds of hope', 86, 89
  South Korean travel projects, 117
  See also Yang, Ching-Ja
Kim, Hak-Sun, 67
  1991 press conference, 87, 88, 101
  first comfort woman, 87, 88, 100, 101, 106
Kim Il Sung, 96
kimoi ojisan, 41
Kim, Puja, 9, 95, 98, 100
Kim, Yeong-Hee, 100
Kitahara, Minori
  academic and activist feminists, 8
  Ajuma Books, 18, 114, 115, 117
  and Flower demo, 16, 17, 20, 23, 104–106, 116
  and *Kibōtane*, 104, 105
  connection to South Korean feminists, 113, 115

feminist in #MeToo era, 11, 16
Love Piece Club, 18, 19, 114
Kōdō Suru Kai, 70, 74. See also
    International Women's Year
    Action Group
Korean Council, the
    campaign against, 88
    December 2015 Agreement, 89
    Korean Council for the Women
        Drafted for Military Sexual
        Slavery by Japan, 90
    Nihon-Gun 'Ianfu' Mondai
        Kaiketsu Senkoku Kōdō, 89
    Yang China-Ja's connection with,
        87
    See also Yoon, Mee-Hyang
Korean resident, 96. See also zainichi
Kuk, Jihye. See Yeolda Books
Kyōfukai, 12, 20

L
Lee, Na-Young, 113
Lee, Yongsu, 87, 88
legal advisor, 57, 58
legislative amendments, 31, 32
Liberal Democratic Party, 29, 32, 33, 36
Lighthouse, 36, 43, 113
lobbying
    importance of, 37
    legislative change, 29
    Spring, 29, 32, 33
Losing Myself at Age 13, 29, 36
Love Piece Club, 18, 19, 114

M
MacKinnon, Catharine, 5, 59, 60, 62, 64, 70, 110, 114
Madonna Boom, 72
Makino, Masako, 3, 23
Matsuo, Akiko, 23

media
    as social education, 74
    foreign, 118
    leftist, 18
    liberal, 91, 92
    mainstream, 17, 18, 91
    right-wing, 72, 88, 92
    social, 5, 16, 21, 25, 49, 74, 105
    See also journalists
#MeToo
    and comfort women, 8, 87, 115
    in Japan, 2, 4, 5, 8, 11, 16–18, 24, 33, 87, 115
    in Korea, 8, 112, 115
Michida Mitsuko, 62
Mies, Maria, 110
Ministry of Justice
    advisory council on sex crimes, 30, 35
    commission into sexual offence penalties, 29
    fact-finding working group, 31
    Penal Code amendments, 61
Miss Tokyo, 77, 78
Mitsui, Mariko
    and Femigiren, 70–72
    and Kōdō Suru Kai, 70
    gender quotas, 72
    Japan Socialist Party, 71, 72
    Norwegian politics, 71
    sexual exploitation, 70, 71
    sexual harassment, 8, 70, 71
    Steppu, 72, 73
    Tokyo Metropolitan Assembly, 71, 72
    Toyonaka City Council, 72, 73
Morita, Seiya, 7, 43, 110
My Heart is Not Broken Yet, 86, 103

N
Nakajima, Michiko, 74
Nakajima, Satomi, 76

Nanmin Kōkōsei: Zetsubō Shakai wo Ikinuku Watashitachi no Riaru, 41
Nihon No Feminizumu Since 1886, 11, 12
Nitō Yumeno
  Joshi Kōsei no Ura Shakai, 42
  Nanmin Kōkōsei: Zetsubō Shakai wo Ikinuku Watashitachi no Riaru, 41
  photo exhibition, 40
  responsibility of adults, 40
  sex industry, 40, 41
  See also Colabo
non-regular work, 111
non-regular worker, 34, 35, 83
'nth-room', 112, 118

O
Ogawa Fumi, 23
Ogawa Tamako, 23
Okinawa, 114
One too alliance. *See Wan Tsū Giren*

P
pandemic
  effect of, on Collabo bus café, 44
  female suicide, 6, 34
  relief funds to sex industry, 113
  restrictions, 23
  sex-differentiated impact of, 6
  'women's recession', 34
PAPS
  collaboration with the Korea Cyber Sexual Violence Response Center, 111
  edited volume about, 20
  Kitahara's involvement in, 20
Pateman, Carole, 110
patriarchal, 54
  culture, 25

oppression, 106
Penal Code
  consent standard for sex crimes, 65
  deliberative council, 29
  feminist movement focus on, 66
  Keihō Kaisei Shimin Purojekuto, 36
  sex crimes amendments, 29, 30
  sex offence provisions, 16
  sex offences amendment bill, 30
People Against Pornography and Sexual Violence. *See* PAPS
police
  domestic violence reports, 6
  Itō, Shiori, 4
  Kitahara's detention, 19
  training, 30
pornography
  child, 7, 117
  DVDs, 21
  fight against, 76
  for women, 20, 21, 118, 119
  in convenience stores, 20–22
  industry, 113, 117–119
  in magazines, 20–22
  in South Korea, 112, 113, 117, 119
  Kabukicho, 117
  legalised, 118, 119
  'revenge', 111, 112
  spy-cam, 112, 119
  trafficked, 110
  United Nations Special Rapporteur on the Sale of Children, Child Prostitution and Child Pornography, 114
  See also PAPS
Poruno Kaishun Mondai Kenkyū Kai, 54
poverty, 6, 34, 78
prostitution
  anti-, 43, 113, 114, 117
  as crime, 51, 113, 117
  child, 7, 42–45, 117

'compensated dating', 42
Kyōfukai, 12, 20
  in South Korea, 5, 105, 113, 117
  'I Was Bought', 40, 44
  'sex work', 43
  survivors, 113, 117
  See also PAPS; sex industry
Prostitution Prevention Law, 5
public molestation, 41

Q
Q no Kai, 81. *See also* quotas
quotas
  against female (university) applicants, 17
  and *Femigiren*, 71, 72, 80
  in politics, 72

R
rape
  consent, 2, 112
  crisis services, 4
  father of daughter, 16, 23
  fujo bōkō, 67
  gōkan, 67
  in law, 56, 57, 61
  'I Was Bought', 48
  legal definition of, 61
  media reporting of, 67
  rice-ball, 42, 48
  threats, 78
  victims, 28, 33, 57, 59, 61, 67
rice-ball, 42, 47, 48
Rokudenashiko. *See* Igarashi, Megumi
Routledge Handbook of East Asian Gender Studies, 10

S
Sakamoto Nanae, 76
Salim Center, 43, 113

Science Council of Japan, 65
scouts, 40, 42
Seibōryoku no Nai Shakai wo Tsukuru Giin Renmei, 32
Seibōryoku to Keihō wo Kangaeru Tōjisha no Kai, 30
Seiji Bunya ni Okeru Danjo Kyōdō Sankaku no Suishin ni Kansuru Hōritsu. *See* candidate gender equality law
Sei to Hōritsugaku, 54, 62
separate surnames, 32, 82, 83
sex
  buyers, 42, 45, 50
  crime, 16, 23, 29, 32, 35, 56, 62, 65, 112, 113
  goods, 18, 22
  industry, 18, 19, 40–42, 45, 105, 112, 113, 117, 118
  inequality, 3, 8, 63
  offence, 16, 30, 54, 68
  offenders, 2, 66
  shop, 21, 22
  tourism, 77
  toy, 18
  trade, 12, 22, 49
sex crime
  acquittals, 16, 23, 32
  amendments, 29, 30
  provisions, 29
  See also Penal Code; rape, victims
sex industry, 18, 19, 40–42, 45, 105, 112, 113, 117, 118
sexual
  abuse, 4, 7, 19, 22, 23, 28–31, 33, 35, 37
  assault, 2, 7, 16, 23–25, 28, 29, 31, 58, 59, 66, 70, 105–107
  discrimination, 21, 22, 25, 56
  exploitation, 8, 12, 42, 45, 47, 49, 63, 70, 71, 76, 77, 105, 118

harassment, 4, 5, 8, 17, 34, 41, 54, 56, 59–64, 66–68, 70, 71, 79, 115
violence, 4, 5, 8, 12, 17, 22, 24–26, 30–32, 34–37, 43, 47, 56, 58–60, 64, 65, 67, 68, 91, 94, 115, 118. *See also chikan*; rape, victims
sexuality
  as a feminist focus, 8, 9, 19, 66
  male, 4, 20
  women's, 18, 21, 22, 61, 62
Shiawase Namida, 37
Song Shin-Do, 97
  court actions, 86, 103
  death of, 103
Sora.net, 112, 119
South Korea
  democracy, 107
  feminism, 6, 8, 94, 105, 112–115, 117, 120
  feminist achievements, 112
  feminist collaboration with Japan, 111
  feminist movement, 2, 3, 6, 9, 105, 114, 115, 117, 118, 120
  women's movement, 106, 107
South Korean Council for Justice and Remembrance for the Issues of Military Sexual Slavery by Japan. *See* Korean Council, the
speaking out, 16, 17, 25, 33, 35, 91, 115
Spring
  as a feminist organisation, 29, 37
  lobbying, 29, 33
  Penal Code reform, 34
  politics, 36
  See also Yamamoto, Jun
Steel, Gill, 3
Steppu, 72, 73
suicide, 6, 23, 34

survivor
  comfort women, 24, 67, 86–89, 92, 100, 101, 116, 117
  Itō, Shiori, 4, 16
  support organisations, 43, 92

T
Taegu Mungchi, 113
Takei, Takako, 80
tea, 75, 76, 79
TENGA, 22
Tokyo Medical University, 17
Tokyo Metropolitan Assembly
  Miss Tokyo, 77, 78
  Mitsui Mariko's election to, 71, 72
  sexual harassment, 71, 79
Tokyo Olympics, 118
Tokyo Rape Crisis Center. *See* TRCC
Toyonaka, 72, 73, 81, 82
TRCC
  as a 'rape crisis' organisation, 60
  connection to America, 57, 58
  legal advisor, 57, 58
  Tsunoda Yukiko's donation to, 56
  victim hotline, 58
Tsunoda, Yukiko
  Flower demo, 54
  Kitakyūshū, 54
  legal advisor, 58
  Meiji University, 54
  Poruno Kaishun Mondai Kenkyū Kai, 54
  sex offence provisions reform, 54
  See also TRCC
Twitter
  attacks, 44

U
Ueno, Chizuko, 10, 42, 95–97

V

Vagina Monologues, 17
VAWW-RAC. *See* Violence Against Women in War Research Action Center
Violence Against Women in War Research Action Center, 86, 113
Voices From the Japanese Women's Movement, 9

W

WAM. *See* Women's Active Museum on War and Peace
Wan Tsū Giren, 32, 36
War and Women's Human Rights Museum, 105, 113
Watashi Wa Kawareta. See 'I Was Bought'
#WeToo, 5, 23
#WithYou, 24
Women in the New World International Network (WINWIN), 81
Women's Active Museum on War and Peace, 7
women's libber, 83
women's liberation, 83, 95, 97
women's liberation movement, 83, 95
Women's Studies Association of Japan, 8

Y

Yamamoto, Jun
 advisory council, 28, 30
 age-of-consent, 28
 Flower demo, 8, 16
 Losing Myself at Age 13, 29
 Penal Code sex crimes amendments, 29
 survivor, 8, 16, 28, 29
 trauma, 28, 29
 See also Spring
Yamashita, Yeong-ae, 98
Yang, Ching-Ja
 connection to the Korean Council, 87
 interpreting work, 87
 My Heart is Not Broken Yet, 86
 response to attack on Yoon Mee-Hyang, 87
 seeds of hope, 86, 89
 Violence Against Women in War Research Action Center, 86, 113
 zainichi, 86, 111
 See also comfort women; *Kibōtane*
Yeolda Books, 116
Yoon, Mee-Hyang, 87, 88
Yoshimi, Yoshiaki, 87
Yoshitake, Teruko, 74

Z

zainichi
 feminist groups, 111, 112
 Kim, Puja, 98, 100
 linking of with comfort women issues, 87, 99
 women, 98–100, 107
 Yang, Ching-Ja, 86, 87, 111
 See also Korean resident

The manufacturer's authorised representative in the EU is Springer Nature Customer Service Centre GmbH, Europaplatz 3, 69115 Heidelberg, Germany. If you have any concerns regarding our products, please contact ProductSafety@springernature.com

Printed and bound by CPI Group (UK) Ltd, Croydon, CR0 4YY

25/03/2026

02078179-0011